Ronald Reagan Speaks Out

"They say that man in his entire history has written about four billion laws, and with all the four billion, they haven't improved on the Ten Commandments one bit."

"You cannot interrupt a pregnancy without taking a human life."

"We have a pledge to Israel for the preservation of that nation."

"I don't want people who practice situational ethics. I would want people who abide by principle."

"I think we've suffered that which Cicero called 'the arrogance of officialdom.'"

"I think there is a hunger in this land for a spiritual revival. A return to a belief in moral absolutes. The same morals upon which the nation was founded."

REAGAN
IN PURSUIT OF
THE PRESIDENCY–1980

REAGAN
IN PURSUIT OF
THE PRESIDENCY–1980

Doug Wead—Bill Wead

haven books
A division of Logos International
Plainfield, N.J. 07060

REAGAN IN PURSUIT OF THE PRESIDENCY—1980
Copyright © 1980 by Logos International
All rights reserved
Printed in the United States of America
Library of Congress Catalog Card Number: 80-52399
International Standard Book Number: 0-88270-466-4
Logos International, Plainfield, New Jersey 07060

Dedicated to Dexter and Birdie Yager.

Special thanks to Judy Ermold, our
secretary, and to members of the
Reagan campaign staff for provid-
ing key documents and accessibility
to the candidate.

Contents

REAGAN
IN PURSUIT OF
THE PRESIDENCY–1980

The Reagan Phenomenon

There is a little of the Churchillian magic in Ronald Reagan's political career. In 1964 he jumped on the very cause which the nation was rejecting. For two and a half decades, Reagan stubbornly held to his view of the world and, while he has yet to receive the dramatic personal vindication of the old Briton from Chartwell, he can indeed make a legitimate claim to a fat "I told you so."

In the 1960s, when Keynesian economists spoke *ex cathedra*, Governor Reagan warned of storm clouds, calling for the federal government to balance its budget or face a day of "unheard of inflation."

In 1966, at a time when America was dancing into the Vietnam debacle, and old liberals like Hubert Humphrey were being touted before us as bona fide patriotic hawks, Reagan brought up MacArthurian fears of a land war in Asia. "We had better fight this one to win or stay out," the Governor said. No one listened.

When the *Pueblo* was seized from neutral waters and Americans were taken hostage, Reagan was troubled. At his weekly Sacramento news conference, the California Governor wondered aloud about the value of citizenship in a country that "won't stand behind you when you're in trouble."

Sensing a warmongering Reagan gaffe, the reporters pounced. "And what is the bottom line?" they asked. "How many hostage citizens should it take for the government to go in and rescue them?"

"Well, it seems to me," the California Governor answered, knowing full well that the reporters present would view any answer as controversial, "that one citizen should be enough."

That's vintage Reagan and, while his detractors thought it risky or provocative, one can easily understand why millions of Americans yearned for the kind of national respect Reagan called for.

Sitting in the coffee shop of the Tehran Intercontinental Hotel during the first weeks of the Iran crisis, one often heard the comment, "Can you imagine what would have happened if they had tried to do this to the Soviets?" Which is the whole point of the Reagan view. They didn't do it to the Soviets. They wouldn't even try. Far from being risky, a blunt legalistic policy presents predictability and order to the world. Indeed, the on-again, off-again style so characteristic of U.S. foreign policy in the late seventies proved exceedingly dangerous. Americans accepted that kidnapped businessmen in South America, cultural centers burned to the ground in Asia, unrepaid foreign loans and citizens taken hostage were all part of being an American. It is ironic that in the name of "cautious restraint" and "sanctity of life" so many had to be sacrificed.

But even beyond such dramatic themes, the most consistent and famous line of the Reagan philosophy has been his crusade against big government. At a time when the Washington establishment was expanding at the rate of 150 percent per year, and every pressure group in America was opting for its share of what appeared to be the "free spoils," the Governor of California was warning that Americans would pay. They would pay with their money, with their privacy, and, choked by endless government regulations, citizens would even pay with their personal liberty.

Twelve years after Reagan began his crusade, Jimmy Carter, a Democratic newcomer to presidential politics, upset the power brokers of his own party and defeated a Republican incumbent by issuing a call for "less government."

But in the summer of 1979, when the Reagan staff was making plans for a run at the presidency, there was a growing suspicion of the "send a message to Washington" or "throw the bums out" theme. That's exactly what the country had thought it had done by electing Jimmy Carter. "They're all the same when they get into office" was the current perception. There was a decided trend toward political apathy.

Ronald Reagan had succeeded remarkably well as Governor of California. He left his successor a multi-million-dollar surplus. This was no small administrative feat when one considers that if California

4

were a nation she would have had the eighth largest gross national product in the world. And, contrary to wild charges by the radical left, when Reagan took the oath of office, policemen did not go around beating people over the head. The world did not come to an end, nobody on welfare starved to death, and West Coast educators who feared the Governor's "no nonsense" approach to student demonstrations found themselves with more state money and less state control than ever before.

Still, in spite of the California record and in spite of national polls which showed a year-by-year trend toward Reagan's own political philosophy, there was not much of a letup in the anti-Reagan lobby of the extreme left. Ultra liberals, sounding much like their extreme right-wing counterparts of yesteryear who thought the election of John Kennedy meant an end to freedom, continued to voice great alarm at the prospect of Reagan coming to power.

A minority of critical newsmen and political opponents generally tagged Reagan as being "dangerous because he gives simple answers to complex questions and issues," which was, of course, itself a simple answer to a complex issue. Reagan had not just postulated a political philosophy, he had enacted it. To dismiss his philosophy as "too simple," without showing why or without wading through the reams of legislative and administrative documentation of his two terms as the Governor of the largest state in the Union was not intellec tually honest.

Yet there was a tendency for Reagan's detractors to cloak themselves in just such political clichés with the result that by the time the 1980 election appeared on the horizon, there had been little substantial discussion as to whether the Governor's ideas would indeed work nationally or whether he had been only "lucky" during his remarkable two terms in California.

There was another problem; many of the so-called "dangerously simple solutions" the Governor had espoused for years were suddenly, in 1980, openly embraced and executed, sometimes by the very political opponents who had once ridiculed them. Balancing the budget of California in 1966 had been called "irresponsible." No one knew what would happen. By 1978, the leader of the Democratic machine which feigned such fear of Reagan belt-tightening was himself calling for a constitutional amendment to bring the federal budget into line as well.

The dilemma had never really been that Reagan's answers were "simple" as much as the fact that they were stated simply. It was his ability to communicate, perhaps a spillover from his glamorous Hollywood days, that stirred the controversy.

When one heard Reagan speak, it made sense. His conversation was riddled with illustrations, the kind that an ordinary person could identify with. People just weren't used to politicians who spoke in English, and intellectuals were sometimes downright suspicious of anything they understood. When one left a Reagan interview, one could actually remember things he said. His positions lacked the ambiguity one had come to expect from politicians.

And so it was that in the fall of 1979, faced with an electorate quite cynical of personalities and quite tired of politics as usual, Ronald Reagan and his staff huddled together to see if they should make the race. It was the last exit before entering the toll road.

He was, no doubt about it, an ideologue. Which was another reason why he made sense. His views had a common philosophical thread. The problem being that the American people had seldom elected an idealogue to the presidency. Thus, they had chosen Taylor, Fillmore, Pierce and Buchanan before taking the radical and controversial step of electing Abraham Lincoln. Still, it was the ideologues, the Lincolns, the men with passionate causes, who had been carved on Mount Rushmore.

The so-called moderate, on the other hand, had often disappointed the electorate. For one thing, it is a blatantly egotistical position. "Let me decide when to be liberal and when to be conservative." For another thing, some isses offer little room for compromise. It is hard to say "maybe" about federally funded abortions. To place trust in a man whose greatest political cause is his own personal attainment of power, no matter how moral or patriotic the man may in fact be, is a corruptible situation.

Ronald Reagan's task was gargantuan. He would have to beat a sitting president. He would have to beat a political machine twice as large as his own. He would have to speak to the electorate via a press and media establishment which had been, in recent history, ideologically antagonistic toward his views.

The polls showed that an overwhelming majority of the American people shared the former California Governor's views. Reagan's gubernatorial record demonstrated he would deliver what he so idealistically called for. But the polls also showed that the American people were disillusioned with the notion that anybody, including Reagan, could bring the mighty bureaucracy under control. A full 60 percent had decided it didn't matter who was elected.

The former American movie star and Governor of California, Ronald Reagan, had to convince the American people one more time that inflation was caused by government, that a strong America would not be shoved around, that federal bureaucracy could be reduced, and that, unlike the unfulfilled promises of candidates before him, he could deliver. The question was, would the American people try for it one more time?

1

The Decision to Run

Pacific Palisades is the ultimate in southern California suburban living. Quiet avenues wind their way gently through the rolling bluffs curving toward unexpected, spectacular views of the sun flashing off the Pacific in the distance. Streets are framed in a healthy green of palm and eucalyptus swaying ever so gently in soft ocean breezes. Large, rambling ranch-style homes of wood, stone, and stucco seem to melt away into carefully manicured yards and gardens that surround them.

There is none of the ostentatious show of new money so visible in nearby Brentwood. The heavy iron gates, stone walls, and private guards protecting the estates of the very rich are to be found in the adjacent community of Bel Aire, not here in the Palisades. The flashy sports cars and show business attitudes so evident on streets in Beverly Hills are rarely seen among the conservative but expensive sedans in this residential area of prosperous family life.

Pacific Palisades, like the people who live there, speaks of the best in the American dream: style, safety, security, and above all, comfort. A comfort that is the reward of a life spent in hard work, a dream realized by the self-made man. This is the community in which Ronald and Nancy Reagan make their home.

Perhaps more than any other single couple in American life, the Reagans have been exposed to the contrasts of their country. Nancy grew up in Chicago, her father a successful neurosurgeon. It was in Hollywood, years later and thousands of miles from their common childhood state of Illinois, that she met her husband. But if Nancy came from a wealthy, urban family, Ronald "Dutch" Reagan sprang from rural poverty. Born in Tampico, Illinois, a little town with dirt streets, the future Governor of California enjoyed no luxuries, and there was no money. His Irish father, John Edward Reagan, sold shoes for a living while Ron clung to a job as a lifeguard or hitchhiked from town to town, looking for radio work. As a young man, he absorbed the full blast of the depression, finally landing a job as a sports announcer; and when he began to rise to stardom in Hollywood, he served as the officer of his union.

It was a life filled with rich experiences and contrasts. When the Reagans finally decided to enter government, their ideas and political philosophy had been finely tuned. It was through hard work, initiative, and sacrifice, that Ronald Reagan had climbed out of the despair and poverty of his childhood years. It was with full confidence and sincere faith in the American dream that he believed he could make a difference.

As Governor of California, he had. But in November of 1979, after two previous runs for the presidency, Ronald Wilson Reagan believed his greatest contribution was still ahead. Arguments against his age notwithstanding, the suburban Californian was about to announce that he would seek the Republican nomination for president.

It was Monday, November 5, 1979, the very week of Reagan's announcement. The Governor, wearing a sports coat with a trim, Ralph Lauren taper, stood in the doorway of his home, greeting his guests for the evening. "Nancy has laryngitis." Nancy was there, right at his side, expressing a little frustration at not being able to do much more than whisper.

Inside, waiters and waitresses in uniforms scurried about the kitchen. I wandered into the library . . . to check out the Governor's reading habits, having only a moment to glance at the tall, black bookcases before another guest followed me in. We were soon chatting away.

A moment later the Governor himself joined us, receiving our compliments on his home but, in self-deprecating humor, insisting that Nancy get all the credit. His love was his ranch, he said. "You know, now that I have a farm they send me the Sears catalog. And I must confess I'm impressed. There's such a wide variety of consumer products available through that one company; we ought to send every Russian a Sears catalog."

A tall waiter served us a non alcoholic, spicy tomato drink with a celery stick, and we were suddenly joined by a fourth guest. "Did you see the Roger Mudd interview last night, Governor?"

Reagan smiled. It was November, 1979, and the polls showed clearly that Massachusetts Senator Edward Kennedy would unseat the incumbent Jimmy Carter as his party's presidential nominee. It would be Reagan against Kennedy in 1980. Roger Mudd had interviewed the senator about Chappaquiddick. In that morning's *Los Angeles Herald Examiner*, Patrick Buchanan had written, "While not hostile, Mudd's questions were direct, probing, personal, professional."

"Well, to tell you the truth," the Governor said, "Nancy and I were so tired last night, we watched for a while from bed and fell asleep." There was a round of laughter and more talk about Chappaquiddick, which the Governor seemed to want to avoid. At one point he graciously calmed one of his guests about the subject, suggesting that President Carter's people would probably explore that issue.

I had just returned from Cambodia the previous day, and Reagan jumped into the subject quickly. The survivors of Pol Pot's reign of terror were arriving by the hundreds of thousands at the Thai border. Cambodia was one place where Marxism had failed in a big way, and the descriptions of starving children brought tears to Reagan's eyes.

"What can be done?" he asked and then commented on the whole tragedy of Southeast Asia. "That was a senseless war. Too many shed blood. We fed our men into a meat grinder. We should never ask our boys to enter a war we don't plan to win!"

I was intrigued by the apparent differences between the Reagan camp and the famous Republican shadow, Secretary of State Henry Kissinger. Reagan talked about the Nixon-Ford foreign policy awhile, and then I brought up the rather complicated apologia of the Kissinger record that was making the rounds at the time.

The former secretary of state often referred to the "substance" and the "appearance" of an agreement and how a negotiator could add a little to one and subtract from the other as a part of the compromise. Thus, the Americans actually could be given a "good deal" by the Soviets but must sacrifice their slight advantage in substance by drafting the communiqué so that the Soviets would gain the "appearance" of a win. According to the theory, the apparent winner could thus use his "victory" for domestic political purposes or even for psychological and foreign policy propaganda purposes. The rationale was that America really did quite well in many of her Kissinger-led negotiations, sacrificing weapon systems she had no intention of developing but allowing herself to appear to be the loser as a concession to the Russians.

Amazingly enough, this was all taken with straight faces, until a nearby Reagan aide jumped into the conversation, suggesting that Americans would be foolish to accept one man's word that we had won a negotiation when it couldn't be demonstrated on paper. The others quickly agreed.

Nancy Reagan rescued us all from the conundrum. She approached the fringe of our huddle with my wife, Gloria, in tow. "She has laryngitis, too," Nancy whispered, bringing laughter. And it was true; perhaps it was the cool ocean breeze—Gloria was losing her voice.

We wandered together on a mini-tour of the Palisades home, admiring a portrait of

Nancy and a Norman Rockwell of the Governor. The caterers brought out steaming dishes, and the party was soon arranged into a line around the dining room table. Guests took spoonfuls of Oriental chicken over rice. There were salads and fruit trays and light yogurt with a whipped cream pie dessert.

Nancy was floating about now, reassuring the guests and, in spite of her laryngitis, rifling off mute signals to the caterers. She was elegant, wearing a long, black velvet dress, fitted to show her tiny waist.

Inevitably, the evening's discussion turned back to politics, and I asked the Governor about his competition in the upcoming campaign.

"The only one I fear is 'Big John' Connally," he answered.

"What about a Republican Jimmy Carter?" I asked. "Reporters assigned to the beat have a vested interest in a close contest. They just might give somebody a little visibility to keep it interesting."

Reagan smiled his predictably good-humored smile. "It could happen. Who do you think they like?"

I referred to a paragraph in *U.S. News'* *Washington Whispers* on the "well organized" Bush campaign in Iowa. The former CIA head had evidently already beat Howard Baker in a straw vote contest in Maine. "Maybe Bush will be the new bandwagon that some of the television people will jump on."

"It's a possibility." The Governor was clearly not too worried, but the more he thought about it, the more he wondered at the impact of television reporting. "You know, the Democratic primary victory of Henry Jackson in Massachusetts last time was a tremendous upset," Reagan said. "But somehow it didn't strike the press as much of a factor, and the Jackson money and momentum just trailed off."

Outside of "Big John," who had reportedly amassed a sizeable financial campaign war chest, it didn't seem that Bush or anybody else threatened the Reagan camp. I wondered at such confidence. In recent years, presidential elections had seldom turned out the way they began. Especially ominous was the power struggle even now ensuing among his entourage. The question that nobody was asking as we stood chatting with the Governor was what was happening to the unity of his own campaign?

With the nomination almost assured and the prospects of occupying the White House looking extremely good, the jockeying for offices in the west wing was well underway. The war had already yielded one very powerful victim, Reagan strategist and advisor Lynn Nofziger. If the tough and wily veteran Nofziger could be toppled, no one was safe.

The two behemoths in combat were said to be long-time Reagan associate and public relations genius, Michael Deaver, and that political master of strategy, Washington D.C. lawyer, John Sears III. There was no question that Sears was ascending. The fall of Nofziger had been a signal that even outsiders could spot. Deaver had reportedly looked the other way during this struggle, and now, with the campaign staff stacked with Sears' loyalists, Deaver was thought be in trouble himself.

There was quite a crowd around the Governor by then, and an informal question-and-answer session developed with Reagan taking on everything from price supports for farmers to his views on abortion. He handled himself with skill.

When the evening was over we gathered at the door to say good night. There is a fascinating painting on the entryway wall in the Reagan Palisades home. It is the picture of an old face, quite thin, with a comical but sad Emmett Kelly expression. One by one, the guests passed by the face and to the door, to shake hands with the host and hostess.

Having just returned from Asia the day before, I sympathized with the Reagan jet-set schedule. They would be off to Boston for a fund-raiser, then back to Los Angeles. "Must be a lot of pressure," I said, squeezing Nancy's hand.

Her voice gone, she gave me an exaggerated look of horror, as if to say, "You'll never, never, never know how much!"

In one chair sat Ronald Reagan, tanned and handsome, showing no fatigue from his 5,000-mile journey to Boston and back. In the other chair sat Jim Bakker, host of a religious talk show described by *Variety* as the "most watched" daily television program in America. The fact that Reagan would appear on stage with Dean Martin and Frank Sinatra at a fund-raiser one day and be interviewed by a television preacher the next struck no one as inconsistent. Such were the changing political times. It would be a volatile election year—predictable voter patterns were in transition. Old alliances were breaking up; new power groups existed. The Democrats couldn't count on the unions any more, and the Republicans couldn't count on anybody. The man who would be President would have to discern those changes.

"I've been flying so much," Reagan sighed. "I don't get in airplanes any more. I wear them." There was laughter from some of us on a nearby couch. A young make-up girl swished in front of the bright lights to powder California's most famous face.

Reagan's Los Angeles office was a disaster. Three cameras were crowded into the little room, and cables were strewn everywhere. Power packs and audio mixers were stacked up on one of the Governor's beautiful, mother-of-pearl, Korean tables. There was an audience of technicians, producers, directors, and secretaries, with a few of the Governor's own staff watching on.

Behind Reagan and Bakker, serving as a backdrop for the little improvised television studio, were the Governor's bookshelves. Between the volumes was a picture of Nancy and their son, Skip, with Pope Paul VI. On a marble stand nearby was a bust of Reagan himself. The sculptured bust was the only immodest gesture in the room.

On one wall hung a numbered print of G.G. Bingham's *The County Election*; on another were prints of old England. In corners of the room stood the flags of the United States and California.

I asked the Governor about his concert with Sinatra and Martin, "Is the old rat-pack breaking up?"

Reagan squinted through the bright lights, "No, Frank Sinatra has always supported me. His affinity was for John Kennedy, not especially the others." It seemed to be a point he enjoyed making.

And then the Governor's face lit up. "You know, an interesting thing, Frank told me that he had been a Democrat all his life. He said he supported Hubert Humphrey and other candidates and never got complaints. But since working for the Republicans, he gets hate mail—fans saying they'll never buy another record."

Reagan, whose eyes have a way of disappearing when his smile broadens, was now chuckling. "Of course, I had been a Democrat most of my early years. I said, 'Frank, welcome to the club.' "

"Governor, what are your views on the Equal Rights Amendment?" someone asked, and the red light in front of the television camera came on.

"I'm for equal rights for women," Reagan looked right into the eyes of his questioner, "but I'm against the ERA. It seems to me that we've passed a lot of legislation to correct the situation, and I think it's time to take the decisions out of the legislatures and put them into the courts."

And then the television preacher zeroed in, "Governor, you've probably seen 1976 Gallup polls showing 33 percent of the American population, Protestant and Catholic, are a part of the Evangelical Christian movement; yet they are practically never represented in government. If you're elected president, will you be careful to appoint blacks, Hispanics, Jews, and the most neglected minority of all, the Evangelicals, to key positions?"*

Reagan nodded solemnly. "As far as Evangelical Christians are concerned, there were a number whom I appointed and who worked with me as Governor of

California." Then he started counting on his fingers. "The first requirement will be that the person is qualified, and," the Governor added, "that will include the person's moral fiber. Yes. My appointments will reflect everyone. And rest assured, I feel comfortable around people who believe in God."

"You're the only candidate who favors a constitutional amendment allowing voluntary prayer in schools," Bakker said.

"Atheism is a belief," Reagan answered. "When one woman can force the courts to take away rights of the majority to breathe a simple prayer before beginning their school day, then I think the pendulum has swung too far."

This heavy talk prompted a question about the Jews, and Reagan launched into his now-famous litany on the strategic and moral value of unquestioned public and private support of Israel and his own disillusionment with the U.S. State Department, "which seems to reward our enemies and punish our friends."

I turned through my notes, looking for a Menachem Begin quote. A very close journalist friend had talked to Israeli Prime Minister Begin the day before and had passed on a question about Reagan. According to my friend, the Prime Minister had begged off the record ("you understand"), but then, his eyes, magnified by the thick lens of his glasses, had twinkled brightly, "I would like Reagan very much."

The television preacher shuffled through the papers on his lap and then fired away. It was a highly personal question which demanded the candidate to reveal a glimpse of his own definitive Christian theology. "Who is Jesus?" Bakker asked.

Reagan without hesitation shot right back, "He is who He says He is." And then he paraphrased C.S. Lewis: "Either Jesus is the Son of God or He is the biggest fraud who ever lived. You can't have it both ways. You can't just say He was a great teacher." There was silence in the room.

"I think this country is crying out for a spiritual revival." Reagan looked down at the arm of his chair. "I've got a feeling that if we don't do something now we may be headed toward Sodom and Gomorrah. We may be the generation that sees Armageddon."

As the Bakker interview continued, my eyes wandered to the volumes in the Governor's bookcase. I couldn't read the titles from across the room, but having missed the chance to look through his home library, I was determined to check out the campaign headquarters.

When the television cameras were gone, I lingered in the Reagan office, glancing at the books and mementos which offer such naked clues of a personality. Omar Bradley's immortal quote on freedom sat on a nearby table.

The library included a conservative but scholarly account of social democracy in Britain, *The Future That Doesn't Work*. There was an old volume of J. Edgar Hoover's *Masters of Deceit*, Murphy and Gulliver's *The Southern Strategy*; and then my eyes focused on *Marathon, 1972-1976*.

With the sound of voices in the hallway and the typewriters ticking away in the outer office, I paused for a brief, tranquil moment, skimming various paragraphs in *Marathon*, reading descriptions of Reagan's 1972 and 1976 campaigns for the presidency. And for a moment I was awed by the fact that, already a figure in the history book on the shelf behind him, Ronald Reagan's most significant hours lay ahead. In a few days, that very week in fact, 1,500 loyalists would crowd into the grand ballroom of the New York Hilton to hear Ronald Wilson Reagan announce for the presidency.

*In May, 1978, the Gallup Poll reported that 53.4 percent of adult Americans—or eighty-four million people—have had a lasting born-again Christian religious experience.

2

The Contenders

It was Monday, January 21, 1980, the day of the Iowa caucuses. The former Governor of California and his wife had planned a quiet evening. While millions of Americans everywhere would be tuning in television sets to watch Walter Cronkite, John Chancellor and Frank Reynolds report the results of the first public reaction to the months of speechmaking and hand-shaking, the hours of radio and television advertisements and coverage, Ronald Reagan, unlike his nine opponents, would be serenely viewing the movie *Kramer vs. Kramer* at the home of friends. Seventeen hundred miles away from the glare of television lights, the microphones of newsmen, the tote boards of campaign headquarters and the hordes of volunteer workers, candidate Reagan had planned a comfortable evening.

The early struggles within the campaign staff had been resolved. Public relations czar Michael Deaver was gone, a major casualty of the conflict. Long-time Reagan chief of staff, Ed Meese, had temporarily retreated to the back of the campaign jet. Meese had the ability to lay low during combat only to emerge unscathed after the smoke cleared.

Public and private polls had shown the campaign strategy devised by chief lieutenant John Sears III would be effective in carrying the first test for Reagan. There was now a definitive plan to capture the nomination and win the general election. The Governor was beginning to feel the confidence exuded by his aides. He was the front-runner. The only way he could lose the prize would be by refusing to take it. Iowa was the heartland of the nation. This was Reagan territory. The people knew where he stood and why. The state was covered by an organization staffed with supporters of long standing who knew how to get out the vote. There had been some slippage in the polls after the refusal to join the other candidates in a televised debate on January 5, but the former Governor had held fast to his Eleventh Commandment: "Thou shall not criticize fellow Republicans." While he had only spent a total of forty-five hours in the state, the crowds had been responsive, and recent developments in Iran and Afghanistan had turned the attention of the media toward foreign affairs, robbing the lesser-known opponents of potential coverage and thus enhancing his chances for victory as the best known Republican contender.

While the people of Iowa began to make their way toward the church basements, town halls and school gymnasiums where the precinct caucuses would be held, Nancy and Ronald Reagan edged slowly from their driveway onto a pleasant, tree-lined avenue for the drive to the nearby home of close friends. The importance of the day had not escaped Reagan. There was perhaps a momentary worry that John Connally's last-minute media blitz might pay off or that recent publicity given George Bush might be an indication of something, but no real need to worry. The race was just now to begin in earnest, but he was already a lap ahead.

Less than two hundred miles southeast

of Pacific Palisades lies the exclusive desert community of Rancho Mirage, California. This town is as starkly different from the Palisades as it is in other ways from Grand Rapids, Michigan, former home town of Gerald Ford. Broad roads intersect one another at right angles, seeming to stretch across the flat, sandy soil for miles to disappear in hazy outlines of mountains far away. Cactus planted in beds of wood chips and gravel is far more common than an occasional patch of green afforded by grass grown at great expense. The only relief from the unrelenting year-round sun is that provided by palm trees. Large, starkly modern houses and predominantly tinted glass seem somehow out of place in the surrounding vastness of the California lower desert. Rancho Mirage is where the rich worship the sun and, unlike its residents who are retirees, everything about it is new. Here, facing the green ways of a private golf course, is the home of former President Gerald Ford.

Ronald Reagan was not the only major Republican figure to spend the evening of Monday, January 21, quietly with friends. However, unlike the former Governor, more like a vast majority of Americans, Jerry Ford would be intently watching televised reports on the Iowa caucuses. For months now aides had been encouraging the former president to announce intentions to seek the highest office once again. They told him he was the only one who could possibly defeat Carter. His experience in foreign affairs, his years in Washington, and his near-victory over the current president in 1976, would make him the ideal candidate of his party. Besides, there were many Republicans who were not satisfied with any of the announced contenders and looked longingly upon Ford's brief but healing time in the White House. Then again, he would have to announce soon if he were to run. Many of his old campaign workers and staff were already committed to others. His chief of staff in 1976 was now directing George Bush's race. It would be hard work this time around. The odds against him were long. Still, eighteen days every month he was on the road speaking. His reception was always good, and wistfully he wondered if things in Iran and Afghanistan might not be different if he were still president. Oh, well, no need to decide this minute. One could await results from Iowa.

George Herbert Walker Bush, a man

who has held more political jobs than he
has names, stepped gingerly from a brightly lighted hotel entrance into the dimness
of the Iowa night. The former congressman from Texas, former director of the
CIA, former envoy to Peking, former chairman of the Republican National Committee and former ambassador to the United
Nations felt his presence at a local Des
Moines caucus might win just one more
vote to his cause. It was 7:00 P.M., CST,
Monday, January 21. The weather was
unseasonably warm for an Iowa winter.
Bush's aides had feared there might be a
more sizable turnout than previously predicted that night if the weather held. A
large number of participants would not
necessarily be good for their candidate;
they wanted no surprises. But as he strolled
briskly down that Des Moines street, George
Bush was not worried about weather. His
step was light and springing. He was buoyant. Dressed in his Brooks Brothers suit,
white shirt and dark tie, face aglow, eyes
dancing and smile gleaming, the former
congressman was the picture of success.
Tonight was to be his night, he could sense
it. He could feel it in his bones. The worst
was over. The long, hard pull was behind

him. From now on he was going to have fun. A strong second place to Reagan would break him away from the pack. Already as he walked, he was aware of the attention he now drew. Television lights flashed, cameras clicked, reporters hastily thrust microphones before him, questions flew. The recognition felt good. Momentum was swinging his way.

The Bush-for-President campaign began in Iowa in December of 1978, two years and one month before any Iowan could officially express his preference for a presidential candidate. Lifting a leaf from Jimmy Carter's notebook on how to win a party's presidential nomination, the former CIA director and his longtime friend, Jim Baker, President Ford's 1976 campaign manager, plotted a course for the capture of Iowa's caucuses. For two long and often lonely years, Bush, his wife, Barbara, his sons, Neil, Marvin, Jeb and George, and his daughter, Dorothy, covered the state. No town was too small, no group too insignificant for the consideration of the Bush family. While a national press all but ignored him and polls showed him at best a distant fourth choice behind Reagan, Connally and Baker, the eastern senator's son, turned Texas oil millionaire, shook hands, ate rubberized chicken dinners and spoke to local Rotary Clubs. At each stop his manner, at first guarded and stiff, loosened. His speeches, delivered in dry, dull tones, began to pick up life and spark. As time drew toward the January date which would determine his fate, the ambassador became a more and more effective campaigner. George Bush was beginning to actually enjoy running for the presidency.

While Bush and his family were busy covering ninety-six of the state's ninety-nine counties, Jim Baker and David Keene were quietly building the kind of grassroots organization necessary to success under Iowa's caucus system. By December of 1979 ten full-time workers and coordinators had been placed in sixty-eight counties. Almost $300,000 had been allocated to put Iowa in the Bush column. Even though nationally the media had shown but passing interest in this candidate's activities, his staff was well aware of the power of the local press. Small-town newspapers, the state's radio and television stations, and the powerful *Des Moines Tribune* were kept well informed of the activities of the Bush family. By the time the former ambassador was walking through the balmy night toward a Des Moines caucus site, his staff

and volunteers had identified and personally contacted 13,000 Iowans who promised to attend their local caucus and cast a
vote for George Bush.

Campaign headquarters was momentarily calm. Only out-of-state staff members
and volunteers remained. The Iowans had
all rushed off moments before to attend
their caucuses and voice one more vote for
George Bush. The large room was a shambles, the floor littered with paper. The long
folding tables covered with file boxes con-
taining the cards naming those Republicans most likely to attend caucuses that
night were no longer manned. Only a few
among the banks of telephones were in use
now, an ardent staff member here or there
trying to round up one last supporter or
answer the questions of some concerned
citizen. The stacks of literature, buttons
and bumper stickers were almost all gone;
even one of the huge posters on the wall
had been removed to satisfy the needs of a
follower. It was a good sign. Since the
debate on January 5 there had been an
increasing interest in the ambassador. He
had done well. His experience in foreign
affairs and his thoughtful, measured answers had shown to his advantage. Since

that time, the crowds had grown in size and enthusiasm, volunteers had increased, and response to the staff's thousands of phone calls to Iowa Republicans had been more positive. The sweet smell of success was in the air now. The staff was optimistic. George Bush was going to do well tonight.

There are some politicians whose very presence exudes power. Such a man is "Big John" Connally, former governor of Texas and former secretary of the treasury. John Connally's rise to national prominence was through the rough and tumble worlds of Texas Democratic politics and oil. A protégé of Lyndon B. Johnson, the former governor of Texas won the respect of most Republicans by switching parties while serving as an advisor to President Richard Nixon. In a brilliant move, Connally announced his new party allegiance during the midst of the Watergate scandal. The timing of this decision, when the party's fortunes seemed to be at their lowest ebb, along with his high position in a Republican administration, immediately propelled the Texan into a place of great prominence within party circles. There had been some talk of a try for the nomination in 1976. But in the era of immediate post-Watergate politics, Connally appeared tainted by his close association with Nixon and charges were made, although proved false, that he had accepted a bribe. John Connally decided to wait for 1980.

From the moment of his announcement of candidacy, the former secretary of the treasury was considered to be a major contender for the nomination. He had national recognition. He had support from many influential Republican businessmen. His ability to raise campaign funds was legendary. John Connally was known as an effective speaker and had a broad base of support in the South. Many Republican party leaders and political pundits could foresee a scenario where Reagan would survive the early northern primaries, bloodied and bruised by close contests with the other contenders, only to be knocked out of the race by a strong Connally organization in the southern states. By the Christmas season, 1979, it appeared that the scenario might come to pass. In an unusual announcement, John Connally rejected federal matching funds for his campaign. By refusing approximately $3 million in grants, the Texan removed himself from restrictions attached to federal moneys. He was now free to raise as much money as he chose. Also removed were spending limitations attached to the individual state primaries. Since at that time the Connally coffers held $8 million, some $2.2 million more than Reagan's, the decision seemed wise. While polls had not indicated any dramatic shift in public support for his candidacy as yet, Connally and his advisors felt that a drive based on a series of expensive television ads would enhance his standing with the voters.

Iowa was to be the testing ground for this strategy. Cutting on organization, the former governor of Texas pumped some $125,000 into a media blitz. It was an ill-advised venture from the beginning. One ad left an impression that Iowa's popular Governor Ray had endorsed the Texan. Ray had not, and strenuously objected to airing the political commercial. It had to be withdrawn. It was soon apparent that the remaining advertisements had not been designed to appeal to Iowans. Nothing seemed to work right for the Connally campaign. A forty-hour bus tour for the press corps, designed to show support for the Texan throughout the state, turned into a fiasco so blatantly choreographed that the press it generated was either indignantly negative or ridiculed the naiveté of a man who was supposed to be the most sophisticated politician of ten contenders.

While Ronald Reagan was confidently guiding his automobile through serene avenues in Pacific Palisades, and in Rancho Mirage former President Jerry Ford was tuning in a local news telecast, while George Bush was springing down the streets of Des Moines, a tall, distinguished, silver-haired Texan slumped exhaustedly into another chair in one more hotel room as an aide flicked on a television set. The bluish glow of the picture tube exaggerated the lines of worry and concern etched into the handsome face of John Connally. Tonight was not his night he knew; whatever momentary fears may have assailed Ronald Reagan, "Big John" would not catch the front-runner position in Iowa. That would have to wait. The most the Texan could hope for would be a respectable third-place finish.

It would be difficult to find, in 1980, a

more sturdy example of what is called "presidential timber" in either party, than Howard Baker, U.S. senator from Tennessee, minority leader of the Senate. Baker's credentials were impeccable. He was a proven vote-getter, the popular Republican senator from a traditionally Democratic state. He was a capable leader, an effective director of Republican opposition to a Democratic majority in the Senate. He had, through an even-handed use of compromise and control, welded diverse views and personalities of minority members of the upper house into a cohesive and potent voice far more powerful in influencing national affairs than its numbers would ordinarily ordain. During the dark days of Watergate, Howard Baker had demonstrated to thousands of Americans who had watched the Senate hearings on television, Republican and Democrat alike, an integrity and intelligence in even-handed application of justice rarely seen in American politicians. He had years of experience in dealing with the Byzantine bureaucracy of Washington and was respected by his fellow senators as a bright, creative man and hard worker. With a political philosophy landing him in dead center of the Republican spectrum it would appear that his party could hardly find a more ideal candidate.

This reputation had earned for Howard Baker the respect and admiration of the party's many elected officials; these included Iowa's Governor Ray. With the governor came the kind of state-wide organization that only a powerful local leader can deliver. The apparatus handed to the Tennessee senator in Iowa was second only to that of George Bush.

But some of the very attributes which made Baker such an attractive candidate on paper placed restraints on the time he felt he could allow for campaign appearances in Iowa. The Iranian crisis and the Soviet invasion of Afghanistan had plunged the nation into a period of deep uncertainty over past foreign policy. President Carter was resolved to seek Senate assistance in creating a united front against Soviet aggression and Iranian terrorism.

Baker's presence as leader of the Senate minority was required in Washington. Howard Baker, whose position as a national leader in less critical times might have propelled him to a position as the main challenger of Ronald Reagan, now became a victim of his job. His commitment as minority leader was more important than seeking caucus votes in Iowa.

It was surely not an easy decision for Baker to make. Undoubtedly the backing of Governor Ray and his organization, with an extremely well-conceived and effective television campaign Baker's staff had designed, if accompanied by a heavy schedule of personal appearances by the senator, might well have placed the Tennessean on the top of the heap, but it was not to be. By Monday night, January 21, Howard Baker, like John Connally, could hope for a strong third place showing at best, with maybe an outside shot at the second spot if Ray's organization could produce a miracle.

The press called them the Big Four. Biggest of all was Ronald Reagan, odds-on-favorite front-runner for the nomination; John Connally, Howard Baker and George Bush were the only announced candidates given even a remote chance of derailing what looked to be a Reagan express to the nomination. Wistfully, some Republicans looked toward a late-hour bid by former President Ford, and there had been some quiet activity on his behalf. But in Iowa it would be up to Bush, Baker or Connally to stop Ronald Reagan.

There were other Republican candidates seeking votes in those Monday caucuses. Philip Crane, congressman from Illinois; John Anderson, also a representative from Illinois; Robert Dole, U.S. senator from Kansas; Harold Stassen, thirty-two years past his prime; Benjamin Fernandez, a Los Angeles businessman of Mexican-American descent: These were the Little Five, each one hoping perhaps to break from the pack.

Philip Crane was a striking figure—young and tall with coal-black hair, bright blue eyes and a square-jawed face. He looked more like a Hollywood leading man than a U.S. congressman. He was the first candidate to formally announce his intentions. He had been actively campaigning for well over a year by the time of the Iowa decision. Crane's constituency, however, was the party's conservative element, and in seeking support from this faction, his efforts from the start ran headlong into the foundation of Ronald Reagan's immense popularity among Republicans. It seemed, from the beginning, that Crane's goals were aimed more at establishing a national name and putting himself forward as heir to the Reagan mantle than actually capturing the nomination. An effective speaker, hard campaigner, and unquestionably pure in his conservative philosophy, Philip Crane had, by the close of Iowa campaigning, come close to fulfilling those objectives.

Equally as attractive in a different way as his fellow congressman from Illinois was John Anderson. Silver-haired, distinguished and handsome, Anderson had achieved national recognition through his performance on the House Impeachment Committee during the Watergate scandal. Known by his fellow congressmen as a hard worker and effective legislator, Anderson was the only contender to base his campaign on the liberal elements within the party. He was the only candidate to express any views that differed much from the others. While a concerted effort on his part might have yielded results in the Iowa caucuses, his strategy called for extended efforts later on in eastern primaries where his liberal philosophy might be received more favorably. John Anderson had written Iowa off. His name was available, but he did not campaign in the state.

The roar was deafening. It seemed that the tension and excitement of the close race for the nomination was over. Every delegate was trying to outdo the other by expressing his party loyalty at least a decibel louder than his neighbor. On a platform high above the heads of the throng packed into the Kansas City arena floor, standing in the glow of spotlights, stood the 1976 Republican presidential nominee, President Gerald Ford, and his running mate, Kansas Senator Robert Dole. The wounded war veteran and party stalwart had been rewarded by his fellow Republicans by being selected to represent them as their candidate for the second highest office in the land. Throughout the following months, right up to the November election, Bob Dole had not disappointed his party. A tough campaigner, he covered the country; with his wit and easy charm he won over many votes for the party ticket. It is expressive of the cruelty of political life that three and a half years later the man who was so wildly acclaimed that summer's night in Kansas City would be listed among the party's minor candidates for the presidential nomination. Only the change in a small percentage of votes would have given the senator the vice-presidency of the United States. Instead, here he was with little money, almost no organization, and only a handful of aides traipsing through an Iowa winter, seeking only enough votes to make his campaign respectable. Nearly everyone agreed that his performance during the January 5 debate had been impressive, but Bob Dole, while respected by all for his ability and intelligence, was for some unknown reason nobody's favorite candidate. By January 21, the facts could no longer escape him: He could hope at best for a miraculous fifth-place finish.

So it was, on Monday night, January 21, 1980, as the nation watched on television and thousands more waited for radio and newspaper reports, that the Republicans of Iowa in cars, trucks, buses and on foot, moved toward the meeting places of their precinct caucuses to give the nation its first factual indication of who, of the nine, might be chosen to face the Democratic nominee in a race for the presidency.

3

George Bush Is Out of the Gate

The precinct caucus was scheduled to begin at 7:00 P.M. That was fifteen minutes away, and already most seats were filled. It looked like there would be about twice the number of participants as had been expected. The temporary chairman huddled momentarily with friends and sent them scurrying off in different directions to see if they could round up extra folding chairs to help alleviate the seating problem. By 6:55, only a few extra places had been made. There was no time to look further; things would have to get underway.

As the chairman introduced himself and indicated the order of business to follow, the room, stuffy and overcrowded with every chair filled and people now having to stand, became charged with that electric excitement and anticipation that seems to be generated only by the American political process.

The matter of the selection of a permanent chairman for the evening's meeting was quickly disposed of. The next item of business, the breaking down of the participants into smaller groups, determined by the presidential candidate each individual supported, was not so easily accomplished. The crowded conditions of the room and the confusion this generated turned the simplicity of moving from one corner to another into a complex game of musical chairs. It was a full half-hour before the caucus was once again under control and the chairman was ready to announce the tallies for each of the contenders.

At that moment a babble of excited conversation broke over the room. People turned in their chairs, craning to get a look at the cause of this sudden interruption. Within seconds the wash of television lights flooded the dimly lit, stuffy confines of the meeting place. To the accompaniment of clicking cameras and the astonishment of the packed room, in walked George Bush, surrounded by an entourage of aides and newsmen.

Gamely, the chairman tried his best to restore order in the hall, now a confusion of shouts, applause and reporters' queries. Gradually the uproar subsided enough to allow the caucus to proceed. With an air of dignity and in sober tones, encouraged no doubt by the microphones now present and the pop of flashbulbs, the chairman intoned the results. George Bush, to his complete surprise and total joy, had won the caucus by a resounding vote.

"I'm on cloud nine. You have made my day," he cried to the cheers of his supporters. Then, just as suddenly as he had entered the room, he disappeared, pausing only to flash a smile, wave a hand and quickly in a brief aside ask an aide, "What does all this mean?"

If George Bush had appeared confident to those who accompanied him a half hour earlier on the walk from his hotel to the caucus site, on the return trip his manner could only be described as ecstatic. Pure pleasure was written across his face in bold strokes as he joined his sons to watch the state-wide returns. Only twice that whole Monday evening was the smile erased. Once in the earnest tones of a New

England prep school teacher, he turned to his sons and exhorted, "Okay, boys, now we've got to go in and cover New Hampshire just like we did Iowa."

The second time around, the smile was erased by an appearance on the television screen of his longtime political rival, John Connally, a man Bush had grown to fear and dislike through their associations in Texas state politics and the Nixon administration. In an interview with TV reporters, Connally appeared to belittle Bush's accomplishment that evening. According to a reporter, the former ambassador responded in a manner much more akin to Texas style than New England propriety by jumping from his seat, slamming his palm on the television set he was watching and uttering a four-letter expletive. But even John Connally could not sour the sweet taste of victory in George Bush's mouth. He had done the unthinkable. The lap's lead of the front-runner Reagan had been closed. Momentum, "Big Mo" as he called it, was on his side now.

The housekeeper cautiously entered the room just as Dustin Hoffman, in a rage of pent-up fury, had thrown a glass of wine at

Meryl Streep. Apologetically, interrupting the viewing of the movie *Kramer vs. Kramer*, she explained there was a TV reporter in the next room who wanted to speak with Governor Reagan. Leaving his hosts and his wife, Nancy, to continue viewing the movie, Ronald Reagan walked into the adjoining room. Waiting there was a local Los Angeles newsman of long acquaintance. After expressing regret for having interrupted the Governor's evening, he gave his news. There had been an upset in Iowa. He wasn't sure of the final tallies, but the networks had projected George Bush as the winner in an extremely heavy turnout.

The quiet evening with old friends was over. Grimly, Ronald Reagan caught up on the results. Over five times the number of Republicans had participated in caucuses this year as had in 1976: 115,000 compared to only 22,000 four years ago. The voting had gone for Bush 31.6 percent in contrast to Reagan's 29.5 percent. Howard Baker had come in third with 15.2 percent. Connally had 9.3 percent, Crane 6.7 percent, Anderson 4.3 percent and Bob Dole 1.5 percent. There could be no doubt, in the first test of the long selection process, Ronald

Reagan had lost. Tuesday would be a long day. There would have to be some serious examination of current strategy for the campaign. This year was the Californian's last chance for the nomination. He could not afford to lose New Hampshire. It would be important for any chance at victory in November that his selection as the Republican nominee be based on a broad string of primary victories indicating his acceptability as the candidate of a united party.

Senator Howard Baker just managed a smile while explaining in soft tones, with the barest trace of Southern heritage, that he had survived and survival was not all that bad when there were so many bodies on the battlefield. But in spite of his smile, the senator could not hide the disappointment in his eyes. A little more than 15 percent was not good enough when you had the backing of a state's popular governor and his organization. There would be no such support in New Hampshire. It would be a difficult race. Howard Baker had a lot of ground to make up.

John Connally, hands clasped on the arms of his chair, sat before the television cameras looking every bit the nervous political science professor. The interpretation of events in Iowa he gave in response to reporters' questions, if not uttered in that distinctive East Texas drawl, could very well have been recited in a college classroom lecture on current political affairs. But glaring overhead lights accentuated the pale color and tight lines of fatigue and defeat written across his face. Talk as optimistic as he may about chances in the upcoming southern primaries, the former governor of Texas was sorely discouraged by the voting in Iowa, and it showed. It was not so much his position at the finish, fourth, as it was the percentage, barely nine. He was still in the top four, but his figures were more like those of the Little Five.

Four weeks before the January 21 caucus, the people of Iowa had been literally bombarded by presidential contenders. With only the exception of Illinois Congressman John Anderson, it seemed that everybody's campaign strategy was based on "pulling it off" in Iowa. Undoubtedly the example of Jimmy Carter's surprise four years earlier and his subsequent nomination and election had influenced the planning of the nine Republican aspirants. The national and even international press, determined not to miss the possibility of a good story, had covered Iowa with over 700 people. More than a thousand extra telephone lines were necessary to meet the needs of the media. It would have been difficult not to be aware of the importance the nation and the candidates were placing on the caucuses.

But Iowa in 1980 was no ordinary state. From the beautiful wooded bluffs overlooking the Mississippi River Valley in the East through the rich central farms to the broad Missouri Valley of the West, the state was populated with an unusually friendly and intelligent people. The days of small acreage farming had faded long ago. The chances were that the colorful, potbellied fellow with the wind-burned face, in the Oshkosh overalls and wool jacket, climbing into the mud-spattered old pickup in front of a small Iowa town's Western Auto store, had a degree in agriculture from the University of Iowa and ran a multi-million-dollar farming operation.

The literacy rate in the state at 99.5 percent was one of the highest in the nation.

Iowans were well read and kept informed of current affairs on a local, state-wide, national and international level by other means as well as the brief vignettes pompously intoned by New York newsmen for thirty minutes each evening on television. The *Des Moines Register*, one of the nation's few truly state-wide papers, covered Iowa like a hen covers her chicks and was read daily by almost a quarter of a million subscribers. Boasting a staff of prize-winning and experienced reporters, the *Register* provided more real news than most big city dailies which devote pages to articles on obscure scandals and murders in remote locations, simply to justify the expense of a news bureau in an out-of-the-way place. Pulitzer Prizes in literature and poetry were awarded to professors and writers at Iowa universities far more often than at many Ivy League schools. The University of Iowa's summer writer's workshop was famous among authors all over the nation for its quality and invaluable instruction.

Politically, the state was revealing a complexity and diversity that belied its old image. In the eyes of political managers, midwestern state distinctions had often blurred. No longer. Iowa was not just a "plains state." It was developing the unpredictability and finicky personal tastes of a New Hampshire. The current moderate Republican Governor Ray was just the latest example of a local politician who had learned how to court the state. One could not take the new sophisticated Iowan voter for granted.

In 1980, national candidates for the presidency, suddenly and some belatedly, learned that lesson for themselves.

By Tuesday, January 22, 1980, political pundits began to issue their "medical bulletins" on the ailing Reagan campaign. Less than a month before the Iowa caucuses, the national polls had shown Reagan to be the favorite of Republicans. Thirty-three percent of those questioned were for Reagan, 23 percent were for former President Ford; Connally was third with 14 percent, Howard Baker fourth with 10 percent, and George Bush was favored by a mere 7 percent. But Iowa had changed all that. The press and television commentators were now convinced that the Republican race could become wide open. The next string of primaries were in the East and now it was felt Bush could seriously damage the

Californian's hopes there. While the contest in the East would be followed by those in a series of southern states, many now held that Connally, with his money, could continue to hamper Reagan's drive in at least Florida and South Carolina, leaving the way open for the emergence of a Ford campaign or the takeoff of Howard Baker in the later contests.

But newsmen are a curious lot. It is boring to follow a campaign with nine candidates when it is obvious one will win. Reporters delegated to the various contenders often develop a kinship with their designated man. In an unofficial way, they become members of the team and look for ways to "pump up" their assignment. The hours on a campaign trail can become very boring. Listening to the same speeches delivered time after time, one's interest wanes. Minor offhanded statements by a candidate are blown all out of proportion simply because there is nothing else to report but the same old thing. There was no doubt in anyone's mind, but that the Bush victory in Iowa made many a newsman happy, not for personal or ideological reasons but simply because it made the race more interesting to report. Many of the comments made on the Tuesday following Iowa were colored by nothing more than an excitement in seeing what was once a one-man race become a contest.

The facts, though, were fairly plain to the men who gathered in the Pacific Palisades home of Ronald and Nancy Reagan, on Tuesday, January 22, 1980. John Sears III, Reagan's campaign manager, was not a happy man. He sat quietly, with his head slightly bent, the dark circles under his eyes accentuated by the pallor and puffiness of his face, the result of a long and difficult night. His only movements: puffing on a cigarette, stubbing it out, lighting another. The former Governor, Sears and a number of the Governor's aides were analyzing what went wrong in Iowa. John Sears was uncustomarily silent. Iowa was his report card. It was not good and he knew it.

It was Sears who, through a series of summer coups, had gained the upper hand in Reagan's campaign staff by ousting a number of old-time confidants of the candidate. He had devised and conducted, with the complete support of the contender, a campaign strategy aimed at broadening Reagan's following by moderating his public pronouncements and limiting appearances to make the Governor look more presidential. The decision not to debate in Iowa had been encouraged and supported by Sears. But the strategy had failed, and John Sears had to take his medicine.

Others in the room carefully pointed out to the Governor that personal appearances were now necessary. He would have to hit the campaign trail and hit it hard. He must dispel the talk about his age. The apparatus of the campaign had to be tightened. A lack of communication and disorganization on the field had hampered the Californian in Iowa. Bush was running hard now and could not be considered a pushover. If Ronald Reagan really wanted the Republican nomination, let alone the presidency, he would have to work for it.

The meeting ground on, but gradually a new strategy was worked out and agreed upon. A new man, William Casey, former chairman of the Securities and Exchange Commission and a wealthy New York lawyer, would be approached to help improve communications and organization. More appearances would be scheduled for Reagan, and any future debates would be joined. The meeting broke up with Sears still in command of the campaign, but his once-iron grip on the candidate's apparatus had been lessened.

In spite of all that came to be written or said, it appeared the people of Iowa chose George Bush over Ronald Reagan simply because Bush worked harder to get their votes. Bush spent practically a full day in Iowa for every hour Reagan was there. Yet Reagan was able to come within two percentage points of victory. The decision not to join the other candidates in debate was probably the decisive factor in the Governor's defeat.

The amount of time Senator Howard Baker was able to spend in the state once again played a major role in the final outcome. Baker, reputedly an able man on the stump, supported by Governor Ray, might have drawn enough votes away from Bush to have put himself over the top or at least a close second to Reagan. But he too had remained above the fray, and this year Iowans were in no mood to buy something they hadn't seen in the flesh.

Accordingly, Iowans decisively rejected the Texas swagger and power of John Connally's television bid. The Connally manner and method was said to be out of place, if not out of date. The Iowa results relegated the former Texas governor to the diminished role of a regional candidate regardless of the results of national polls.

The biggest loss in Iowa was that incurred by Kansas Senator Robert Dole. In spite of a bright, witty and intelligent performance in the televised debate, the former vice-presidential nominee could generate little more than 1.5 percent of the vote. Facing a reelection campaign for his Senate seat, friends urged the Kansan to give up the attempt and concentrate on the home front.

Congressman Philip Crane drew 6.7 percent of the vote, somewhat better than expected, although most of the Illinois congressman's votes were attributed to hardcore conservatives. If the congressman were running with the limited ambition of establishing a national name for himself and placing his face before the public as a future successor to the Reagan mantle, he could count his efforts a modest success.

John Anderson, the maverick in the crowd, gathered over 4 percent of the Iowa Republicans' votes without campaigning. It had to be looked upon as a fairly good showing for a man with liberal views who

espoused programs considered traditionally liberal in an election year in a state
where the predominant concerns of the
voters appeared to be far more conservative.

Hotel rooms were available once again
in Des Moines. Here and there one would
run across a large, empty storefront that,
upon closer inspection, revealed among the
dust and debris a marred and deformed
campaign poster of some forgotten presidential contender. The telephone lines had
been pulled. The local press newsrooms
had returned to normal. The farms lay
peaceful. Politicians and reporters no longer trampled across the fields, now sprin-
kled with the green of tender shoots. The
race for the nomination had run through
Iowa; the noise of the contestants was far
away. All was quiet again. Until the next
time.

4

The Race Runs East

Grinding slowly to a halt, the string of cars pulled into the curb in front of the pharmacy. Half a dozen doors slammed, and a group of men hunched against the cold, with their feet crunching in frozen snow, made their way toward the door of the drugstore. A window display of red, plush Valentines and candy in heart-shaped boxes had been sighted by the leader of the group, reminding him that he had yet to purchase a Valentine's Day card for his wife. The pharmacist looked up briefly as the entourage entered, nodded recognition and then returned to his work. This was New Hampshire in February and even in small-town drugstores the appearance of presidential contenders was taken for granted.

The two lady customers at the card rack, however, were not quite so blasé. The tall, handsome, dark-haired gentleman who asked for their assistance in selecting a Valentine for his wife was no ordinary candidate. It was still easy for anyone to see how this man had been a matinee idol. After thanking the ladies for their help and asking for their support in the primary, the Governor was off in the motorcade to one of his many scheduled stops, leaving behind two sure votes in the pharmacy.

The Reagan campaign's response to George Bush's little surprise in Iowa had been to abandon the winter strategy of John Sears and with an alacrity that was nothing less than awesome, to put their man before the voters. What George Bush was able to achieve through photographic sessions and interviews given while jogging, Ronald Reagan had to do by filling a new campaign schedule with so many stops that even the heartiest of the newsmen assigned to him could no longer doubt that this man's stamina, even though he was sixty-nine, was certainly no hindrance to his ability to run a full campaign. The contender was determined to leave no voter in doubt as to whether or not he wanted or needed their vote.

By the middle of February, the former Governor had led the press and his aides on a series of campaign trips that would wear out a man twenty years younger. Beginning immediately after Iowa, the Californian had sent his advance men scurrying across the country to arrange the new schedule with local supporters. Armed with a checklist of over 100 items, so detailed that the height of lecterns to be used by Reagan was specified, the aides, sometimes barely completing the organization of a stop before the candidate's arrival, managed a seven-state tour without a hitch. For a campaign that had only a week before suffered defeat, due in part to a communications problem, the effort was nothing less than spectacular. Plane trips, bus rides and motorcades arrived on time to airport receptions, high school auditoriums and banquets—not a minute was wasted. The audiences were always large and warmly receptive. In his speeches Reagan abandoned the noncommittal platitudes of the winter strategy and returned to his familiar form, calling for a strengthening of defense and a recognition of the dangers of Russian aggression. Bowing to the lesson learned in Iowa, the Governor gamely agreed to debate the other contenders, first in New Hampshire and then later in South Carolina, even though he feared he may be setting himself up for an ambush.

Whether or not the coming debates were to be ambushes for Reagan, he had planned one of his own for the press who had skeptically, since the inauguration of his campaign, nagged about his age. On Ronald Reagan's sixty-ninth birthday, he scheduled a total of twenty-eight campaign appearances: Cutting cakes in Los Angeles; Hooksett, New Hampshire; and Greenville, South Carolina, the "Old Man" led the press around the country on a birthday celebration that would have sent a twenty-nine-year-old to the hospital for exhaustion.

At the close of the seven-state birthday tour, Reagan turned his attention fully on New Hampshire. The polls were now showing George Bush leading there by almost 10 percent (Bush 45 percent, Reagan 36 percent). New Hampshire's primary would be followed by that of Massachusetts in early March, where Bush was considered a sure winner. The Governor had to have a good showing on February 26.

The click of cameras and the whir of tape machines were recording every move and word of the man breezing through the aisles of the New Hampshire department store. Immaculately dressed, calm and confident of manner, George Bush, face beaming, hand extended, refused to miss any possible voter. "No fair hiding. You can't escape. I'm George Bush. I would love to have your vote." More like a successful evangelist seeking souls than a presidential politician, the former ambassador plunged exuberantly through the throngs of shoppers. Brushing past a silent, motionless customer, Bush turned, smile blazing, in a vain attempt to garner the vote of a store mannequin. Briefly nonplussed, he turned sheepishly, grinned at the laughing aides and newsmen, and plunged on.

Ever since the momentum, as he said, had swung his way in Iowa, George Bush seemed to have been having fun. At every stop his crowds were large and enthusiastic, but he would not limit his vote-seeking to school auditoriums and hotel dinners. No hand anywhere in New England was safe from his grasp. In a campaign drive directed state-wide by former New Hampshire Governor Hugh Gregg, Bush was worked so hard his regular daily schedule allotted only twenty-two minutes for lunch. However, very often he was scheduled so tightly that only six minutes were granted the contender in which to wolf down a sandwich. But George Bush did not seem to mind the severity of his days; to the contrary, in public he seemed to thrive on it.

But in spite of his public appearance and the attitude of cheerful confidence, the campaign was beginning to wear on the ambassador. George Bush had been actively seeking the presidency at this time for almost two years. Most of those months had been spent in relative obscurity. He had, until the final weeks before the Iowa caucuses, been almost ignored by the press. The game was different now; he was considered a strong contender and with his increased standings in the polls, came a more careful scrutiny by the media. First in the *Los Angeles Times*, then in William Loeb's powerful Manchester, New Hamp-

shire, paper the *Union Leader*, charges
that Bush had not legally reported campaign contributions from a Nixon slush
fund during the ambassador's unsuccess-
ful attempt for a Texas senate seat were
revealed. Bush was irate. "What the hell
are they bringing that up for now?" he
exploded in anger.

Loeb, a Reagan supporter, continued his
attacks on the former Texas congressman
on a daily basis, bombarding his readers
with everything negative he could possibly
find about the ex-ambassador. But George
Bush had spent his life in and around politics and, except for rare occasions, the
anger, hurt and frustration that comes
with the status of favorite was kept from
the public view.

The house on the golf course in Rancho
Mirage was quiet. The occupant was busy
elsewhere. Busy, indeed, for a noncandidate; speaking to Republicans in Utah and
Nevada, then addressing the convention of
a produce association, former President
Ford was not seeking the votes of New
Hampshire's populace. But he seemed to
be highly visible everywhere else. Responding to an increasing number of reporters'

inquiries, the smiling, tanned, and healthy-looking Ford by mid-February was sounding more and more like a candidate. He was available, he said, "If the ball bounced one way"—"If my party should happen to want me to be a candidate, of course I would accept the opportunity," if any groundswell "is loud enough to be heard." Aides of the ex-president spoke in more specific terms: "We have a base of support." They claimed between 15 and 20 percent without campaigning. But the true word was if Ronald Reagan pulled "less than 35 percent of the vote in New Hampshire," the house on the green way in Rancho Mirage would become a much busier place, and noncandidate Ford just might become candidate Ford.

The weather in late January and through the middle of February was unusually warm for the Ozark Mountain regions of southwest Missouri and northwest Arkansas. The usually gray winter skies were sparkling blue, and the air carried a quality of springtime. The many lakeside resort hotels of the area were, however, not much busier than they might have been had the ground been dusted in the white of snow.

Gasoline prices had offset the effects of good weather. The heavy vacancies made it easy for the campaign staff of Texan John Connally to rent one of the better hotels for an entire weekend. It was there among the sylvan hills on the side of a peaceful lake in the Ozarks that the former governor of Texas courted the favor of the Arkansas delegation to the 1980 Republican Convention.

All nineteen delegates and their spouses, along with various other state party officials, had been invited to the weekend bash of Texas-style barbecue and cocktail parties. It was one of the most elaborate and costly attempts to woo delegates of any contender in the whole of the 1980 campaign.

Since the Iowa caucuses, Connally, like all the other Republican hopefuls, had stepped up the pace of his personal appearances. But while most of the candidates were plodding through the snows of New Hampshire, John Connally was concentrating on the South. There would be a series of primaries in South Carolina, Florida, Georgia and Alabama shortly after New Hampshire, and "Big John" was busy preparing an ambush of Reagan's campaign in Dixie. Since his rejection of federal matching funds, the Texan was no longer bound by spending restrictions, and so he spent and spent freely.

Puerto Rico, holding its first presidential primary on February 17, was another place where the Texan was hopeful of slipping in and stealing the fourteen delegates. Galloping through the streets on horseback, gulping down alcapurria or sipping mavi, the big Texan's smile and manner delighted the Puerto Ricans. Reagan had chosen not to enter the island contest, so Bush, Connally and Baker were in it alone. A victory over Bush, the favorite, in Puerto Rico, coupled by a defeat of Reagan in one of the Southern contests, would propel Connally's campaign forward and more than make up for the disappointment in Iowa.

In the meantime, the other candidates plowed on. Baker, Crane, Anderson and Dole were concentrating like Bush and Reagan on New Hampshire. The scenes were the same for everyone, only the contenders' faces changed. The candidate standing, coffee cup in one hand, gesturing with the other, face animated as he explained to the quiet group of neatly-dressed and proper women sitting in a neighbor's living room why he would make a better president and needed their vote. The high school gymnasiums all looked alike. An American flag hanging from the high beams overhead, clusters of balloons tied to the basketball goals, folding chairs half-empty and the temporary platform, the same for each one of the nine, only the hastily hung campaign posters changed with the man. The entourage moving through the shoe factory, the candidate stopping before a rattling, shaking machine to listen to the instructions, shouted over the clicks, hammers and bangs of manufacturing, on how to make a shoe; as if he failed to win this worker's vote in the primary, he, too, might have to make shoes for a living. So it went for them all. The ritual of pursuing the presidency hardly ever varies. All the contenders must seek out and solicit the vote.

By February 17 Arkansas and Puerto Rico had selected their delegates. Connally's efforts had been to no avail. Bush won in Puerto Rico with 59 percent of the vote. In Arkansas Reagan had gathered nine delegates, but Ambassador Bush had, in the heart of Reagan territory, run off with eight. It was very plain now that New Hampshire's role in the primary process was even more vital than the contenders had first imagined.

And so the stage was set for the first televised confrontation of the seven serious contenders for the Republican presidential nomination. On the evening of February 20 the high school auditorium in Manchester, New Hampshire, was filled to capacity. Throughout the hall, television cameras placed in strategic locations were aimed at the brightly lit stage. Beneath a large banner proclaiming "League of Women Voters' 1980 Presidential Forum," eight chairs were arranged in neat order behind two long, draped tables. By the luck of a draw, the first chair was to be filled by John Anderson. The next by John Connally; then Philip Crane and George Bush completed those at the first table. Seated neatly in the middle was Howard K. Smith, one of those venerable old newscasters who retire from the network's nightly news to become political commentators, pronouncers of truths others have missed and the conscience of the nation. The second table was occupied by Howard Baker, Robert Dole and finally, Ronald Reagan.

It became apparent early in the evening that the only thing saving the debate from becoming an hour of boring "me too's" was the stubborn insistence of the professorially handsome, silver-haired John Anderson, in proposing liberal remedies and expounding ideas with an evangelistic zeal that could only cost him votes among the majority of New Hampshire Republicans.

Otherwise, Philip Crane wore a constant expression of youthful, righteous indignation on his strikingly good-looking and finely chiseled face. John Connally, trying his best to look the experienced, international statesman, ruined the impression every time he spoke. Looks aside, the East Texas drawl of the former secretary of the treasury, regardless of the words, sounded like Lyndon Baines Johnson. George Bush, obviously aware of his new status as front-runner, looked exuberant, smiled a lot and said as little as possible. His aides and his own experience had coached him that in avoiding talk one can often avoid mistakes.

Senator Howard Baker displayed the

same manner which had brought him to prominence during the Senate Watergate hearings by carefully answering the questions or discussing the topics presented in a manner that offended no one. Smoothly, he left each listener sure that the senator's views, if not the same as those held by the audience, certainly were intelligent and well-thought-out. Senator Dole's answers were laced with levity, warmth and the strength of convictions held with intelligence. Of all the debaters, only the Kansan with his humor and sensitivity seemed able to convey a feeling of humanity. It was no secret to anyone in the auditorium or viewing on television that Dole would most likely be the first forced from the race. Yet in spite of the pain and futility of his campaign, there he was with reason and wit, seeking to convince the voter, somehow avoiding the desperation he must have felt.

Ronald Reagan was the last speaker on most issues. By the time it was his turn to respond, he had already heard: a former Texas governor, once a moderately liberal Democrat; a young congressman, who was a recent college graduate when Reagan first drew national political attention; a

former U.N. ambassador, who only a year
before was languishing in relative political obscurity; the minority leader of the
Senate, long considered a moderate; and
the senator from Kansas, Gerald Ford's
former running mate. Each one attacked
the answers of John Anderson, and each
one proposed an alternative based on the
ideals and philosophy that Ronald Reagan
had been campaigning on since his speech
in support of Barry Goldwater in 1964 had
first drawn him to national prominence. It
must have been as amusing to him as it
surely was frustrating to hear these five
contenders adopt and pronounce as their
own policies those that, only four years
earlier when the Governor was contesting
Ford for the 1976 Republican nomination,
they had rejected as too conservative.
Throughout the evening the Californian
was given, at best, only the opportunity to
say, "I disagree with Congressman Anderson and agree with the other five."

Finally, in the inimitable style of a network newscaster, Howard K. Smith
opened the forum to audience questions.
Each question and the contenders' re-
sponses were as decorous as those delivered earlier—until the "one last ques-

tion." It was directed to Ronald Reagan.

Brow furrowed in distress or frustration, a gentleman in the audience stood erect, squarely facing the Governor. Once an earnest supporter of Ronald Reagan, the man was puzzled and obviously stung by a recently publicized story of an ethnic joke the Governor had told a group of newsmen during a campaign trip. Reportedly, Poles and Italians were the subjects of the joke, and the questioner expressed genuine dismay over any slurs possibly directed at members of his ethnic affiliation.

In an effort to allay the man's concern, Reagan indicated that the incident in question had not always been reported with complete accuracy and assured the man that the joke itself, devoid of maliciousness, was told in all innocence. During the long, trying days of the presidential campaign, a candidate often develops close relationships and camaraderie with the reporters assigned to cover him. Not only are these men and women often attached exclusively to the candidate throughout the race, but the contender and the newsmen are thrown together on lengthy bus and plane trips.

Such was the case of Ronald Reagan and

the reporters assigned to him. The affable Californian and the press had established a healthy relationship since the earliest stages of his campaign. To relieve the boredom of tedious, long-distance travel, the pressmen, aides and candidate exchanged jokes and anecdotes. Of course, in compliance with their "gentleman's agreement," anything said during these informal, chatty sessions was strictly "off the record"—not for print.

One listening reporter, however, could not resist publicizing the Governor's joke, and his account resulted in a blowup by a news media hungry for controversy just prior to the debate.

"I'm glad you asked that question," Reagan responded to the troubled questioner. Tension in the New Hampshire debate peaked as the Californian intimated that the topic of conversation during the campaign trip had turned to the tastelessness of ethnic jokes; his might have been considered an exemplification. At this point, one loyal but apprehensive Reagan aide whistled his alarm and sighed in resignation at impending political disaster—"He's gonna blow it!" Even a truth can be hazardous, if it appears contrived.

Perhaps discerning his questioner's dissatisfaction, but not missing a beat, the Governor moved right into a straightforward and humble apology with the assurance he admires both the Poles and the Italians. Furthermore, Reagan quipped, he would look over both shoulders before ever telling another joke, and then tell only Irish jokes, since *he* is Irish. Tension broke, and the reinspired Reagan aide released a hearty sigh of relief.

The moment of that final question was, no doubt, the most embarrassing for any of the participants. And, in forums of this type, the last question and its answer are often the ones remembered the longest. Reagan's response and deft handling of the situation was impressive in its candor and sincerity, and he presented himself as a man who did not duck a sensitive issue with evasive answers. Additionally, this was a completely unrehearsed opportunity, in front of a national viewing audience, for a man whom the press and other media had been portraying as absent-minded and slow in response, to demonstrate his true mental agility.

The media pundits declared the forum a draw. Nobody had lost; nobody had won.

George Bush had not harmed his role as front-runner. No one else had been impressive enough to really enhance his position. However, in spite of what the media might have thought, many people who had never heard of John Anderson before got their first close look at the veteran Illinois congressman. Because his views differed from those of the others, many people began to think about what he had said. And Ronald Reagan, by leaving a good last impression, had managed to cap the lid on an incident which might have caused further embarrassment.

And so the first New Hampshire debate ended. The candidates on stage cordially shook hands with one another, paused for photographs and bent down to sign autographs as the voters, who would determine the fate of each of the seven, filed out of the auditorium into the crisp New Hampshire night or rose from their easy chairs to switch channels to something a little more exciting. Nothing had been decided. There were still six days before the primary, and in presidential politics, six days can be forever.

5

The Great New Hampshire Debate

The Nashua, New Hampshire, high-school gymnasium was sparkling clean. There was not a speck of dust to be found anywhere. The seating available in the bleachers had been supplemented by row after precisely lined row of folding chairs. Extra lights brought in to provide the illumination necessary for television had been positioned carefully around the large room. The cameras to be used for broadcasting the event were in place, their heavy cables neatly covered just enough to provide maneuverability and yet protect the unwary from tripping. A deep blue drape, flanked by the U.S. and New Hampshire flags and crowded by a proud sign proclaiming: *"NASHUA TELEGRAPH*

PRESIDENTIAL FORUM," provided the stage backdrop, in front of which were three tables, neatly curtained in white. At each place was a microphone and chair. All was ready for the second New Hampshire debate.

A week after Iowa's caucuses, the once debate-shy Ronald Reagan had agreed to join the other candidates in confrontations in New Hampshire and South Carolina, sponsored by the League of Women Voters. A few days later, encouraged by his campaign aides, Reagan issued a challenge to George Bush to meet him in a one-to-one confrontation between the two leading contenders. Bush accepted. The local newspaper in Nashua agreed to sponsor the event. The date was set for Saturday, February 23, 1980, just three days before the primary balloting. Then on the Thursday prior to the scheduled debate, the Federal Election Commission ruled that sponsorship of such an event by the *Telegraph* would constitute an illegal campaign contribution. Governor Reagan quickly offered to divide the $3,500 cost with the Bush organization. The Bush campaign, however, felt by now that avoiding the debate altogether might not be such a bad idea. If Reagan really wanted to meet their man head-on, then he could pay the bill. The Californian paid, and so the debate plans continued.

By the morning of the scheduled meeting, Reagan and his staff began to wonder if they had done the right thing by excluding the other candidates. There had been a rising chorus of criticism from the camps of those contenders not asked to join. Hastily, the Governor's aides spoke to the hopefuls then in the state, Baker, Crane, Dole and Anderson, and extended an invitation for them to participate in the forum that night. The four men accepted and agreed to meet at the school early in order to develop a procedure for the evening's meeting.

That night, as the parking lot surrounding the gymnasium began to fill and people filed into the building to watch the cameramen, sound experts and lighting technicians test their equipment, Ronald Reagan, Howard Bush, Philip Crane, John Anderson and Robert Dole gathered in a small room just off the stage. Shortly thereafter, George Bush entered the building. As he was approaching the platform, a Reagan aide invited him to join the others. With his mind distracted by the debate and obviously trying to concentrate on the event, Bush, also perhaps fearing some kind of a trap, declined. He said he would rather use the brief period of time remaining before the debate began to prepare. The ambassador moved on to his place on the stage.

The gymnasium was now filled to capacity. Camera crews and technicians were set. The press were poised. As Jon Breen, editor of the *Telegraph* and moderator of the event, took his seat, the room quieted. All was in place, everything was ready; only Ronald Reagan was missing. The room was charged with anticipation. Bush removed his glasses. Looking up from the notes on the table in front of him, he glanced toward the crowd, at Reagan's empty chair and then questioningly at Mr. Breen. No other glance was necessary. Almost immediately into the room and onto the stage to the desk prepared for him, strode Ronald Wilson Reagan, every inch of his six-foot-one-inch frame looking presidential. Following the former Governor onto the stage came four other contenders: Anderson, Bush, Dole and Crane.

As soon as he was seated, Reagan leaned toward his microphone. Expansively and eloquently he argued for the enlargement of the forum into a six-man debate. Bush, who had some days previously told the *Telegraph* he would have no objections to a forum including all the candidates, looked startled and confused. Saying he was invited by the newspaper's editors, that he considered himself their guest, was happy to be there and would play by the rules, the ambassador left the distinct impression that he was against expanding the two-man debate. And then it happened—one of those odd little twists of fate that change the course of events so often. As Reagan leaned toward the microphone, once again to press his case, moderator Breen, who had been insisting the format would not be changed, ordered the power to be cut off. His jaw set, his eyes aflame, decisive action written across his face, Ronald Reagan grabbed the mike and in barely controlled, determined tones, announced, "Mr. Breen, I am paying for this microphone!"

Behind the gymnasium stage, John Anderson, Philip Crane, Howard Baker and Robert Dole gathered in the glare of television lights. Two United States congressmen, two senior senators, one a minority leader of the Senate, the other a former vice-presidential nominee, their expressions at once incredulous and angry. Like errant schoolboys, they had been summarily dismissed from the proceedings on stage by the editor of a newspaper with a circulation hardly as large as the smallest town in their constituencies. Their anger and rage at such treatment was vented into the assembled microphones thrust into their faces by network correspondents, who had the intuition to know that the little impromptu gathering was not the sideshow but rather the main event. The object of their fury was George Bush.

The forum inside proceeded in all seriousness. It was a two-man debate as originally planned. The four other candidates had left. But the result was academic. What was said or not said, answered or not answered by either man, no longer mattered. Ronald Reagan had won the crucial head-to-head confrontation with George Bush, before the first question was asked, before the first topic was raised. With his impassioned plea for the addition of the other contenders, and most importantly, with his spontaneous display of firmness and indignation in a situation in which his antagonist so obviously played the role of villain, Ronald Reagan had revealed to all who watched a personality characteristic many American voters were looking for in their president that year. Prompt, firm decisions without fear of his opponent. In those brief seconds, the Californian left the impression with all who viewed that this man would back his words with action. Ronald Reagan would never allow our country to be insulted by the Russians or anyone else.

No slick Hollywood or New York film crew could have ever asked for more from their star. It was a superb performance because it was not an act. It was real. Every network in the country picked up the event. Those who had not seen it happen saw it replayed on their evening news. Late that Saturday night and then on Sunday's network shows the incident was repeated, often accompanied by a second film clip of the four nondebaters in which the normally calm Howard Baker angrily denounced George Bush's behavior in not allowing the others to join the debate as the most odious he had ever encountered in politics. By Monday morning at the latest, certainly every New Hampshire voter and most other Americans had heard of or seen the incident. With only two days to go before the primary ballots were to be cast, Ronald Reagan had struck a masterful blow. The race was tightened up.

Exhausted, George Bush returned to his Texas home for two days' rest, immediately following the forum. And so it was that on the Sunday and Monday prior to Tuesday's vote, the people of New Hampshire saw pictures of "the younger" Mr. Bush resting by his pool, and compared them to those of "the older" Mr. Reagan sloshing through the snow, greeting supporters, and still working hard to capture first place on Tuesday.

It was late Tuesday afternoon, February 26, 1980. New Hampshire polls would be closing in a couple of hours, as John Sears III, the brilliant and caustic chief of the Reagan campaign, ambled down the corridor of the Manchester Holiday Inn. Sears had been summoned by the Governor. With hair characteristically tossled and suit rumpled, the campaign director entered the boss's suite. Pausing briefly to stub out an ever-present cigarette, he walked toward the corner where Reagan was seated. Nodding politely to a particularly sad-looking Nancy Reagan, Sears turned his attention to the Californian. John Sears was feeling good. In spite of the mistakes in Iowa, he knew he had done a great job with New Hampshire. The debates had turned out well, and the latest polls showed his man, once a ten-point underdog, to be now even with Bush. The campaign had been saved and was back on track. Handing his campaign chief a piece of paper, Reagan requested that Sears read the news release which was to be issued the next day. In stunned silence, the manager read a press announcement of his own dismissal from the Governor's staff. The Governor also requested the departure of two Sears lieutenants: Jim Lake, press secretary, and Charles Black, national political director. The new campaign manager was to be William Casey of New York. So as not to appear ungrateful of Sears's efforts in New Hampshire, the news was to be released after the results of voting, regardless of the outcome.

It was a difficult decision for Reagan. He had grown to admire and deeply respect the intelligence of his former campaign boss, through the struggles of the 1976 race and even up to the time of Iowa. But after the loss in Iowa, the former Governor began to pay closer attention to details of his operation. What he saw and heard from most of his staff did not reflect well on Sears. Somehow of the $18-million pre-convention spending limit for each candidate, Reagan's campaign had used $12 million, and only the first primary was now finishing.

It is a fact, often overlooked by the press in the 1980 election year, that while he served as Governor of California, Reagan demonstrated a talent for attracting bright men into state service. Once he was satisfied with their abilities, he would unhesitantly delegate vast authority to them. It is a further fact, however, that if the Governor felt that authority to be abused, misused or not effectively used, he would remove the individual, regardless of his personal feelings. Ronald Reagan was never afraid to make hard decisions and, once he made them, to stick to them, in spite of what the public or press might say.

The removal of Lynn Nofziger had been such a decision. So had the confrontation with longtime aide Michael Deaver. In the shadows offstage, John Sears had enthusiastically applauded the Governor in these showdowns. And with good reason, Reagan loyalists were being replaced by Sears loyalists. It may have led the campaign manager into believing that Reagan was only an extension of himself, that the Governor drew his nerve and wisdom exclusively from Sears. Nofziger and Deaver could have told him otherwise. The patient and gracious Reagan was no patsy. Sears was allowed to build his personal infrastructure, but when obsession for control of the Reagan campaign hurt his effectiveness for the candidate, a surprised Sears found himself a casualty. But if he could be strong, Ronald Reagan was also merciful. If John Sears could humbly find a seat in the audience with Deaver and Nofziger, he would probably be called back into service again. But it was not John Sears's style to wait around.

The camera clicked. The picture that all candidates studiously avoid had been taken. Propped in a corner of the couch sat the contender, still in coat and tie, his face momentarily abandoned to the fatigue of failure, eyes intently gazing at the aide bending before him. On the far end of the sofa sat his wife. She, too, had turned her attention toward the aide crouched before her husband. After the long day, somehow immaculately dressed, hair in perfect place, serenely sitting as if waiting to be escorted to her favorite restaurant, but in her eyes that longing, even pleading, look that women can reveal, saying, "Please don't tell my husband what I think you must." The background was completed by the bright, handsome young man, chin in hand, eyes disbelieving, listening to the recitation of facts that nonetheless sounds disloyal to his boss, because they are not what he wants to hear. The aide, the focus of attention, kneeling before the contender in such supplication and humility that one could imagine he feared for his life, the news he was delivering was so bad. Holding a paper in one hand, his head in the other, disappointment stamped on his face, he read the figures confirming the worst.

The balloting had ceased. The votes were being tallied. The once healthy advantage in the polls had disappeared. The neck-and-neck race had on election day turned into a rout. Thus, on the night of February 26, 1980, the Indian Summer of George Bush was blown away by the cold realities of the New Hampshire voter. It had lasted exactly thirty-six days, from the victory in Iowa to the news of defeat in Concord, New Hampshire.

The scene was a familiar one in American politics. The large hotel banquet room festooned with red, white and blue balloons and crepe paper streamers. There was the temporary platform and on the walls, the huge campaign posters and photographs of the smiling candidate; stationed in various locations throughout the room were color TV sets tuned to the different networks, surrounded by little seating sections for viewers. In the back of the room a table was set up for coffee, the large urn steaming beside the rows of neatly stacked styrofoam cups. Up front near the platform, where all could see, would be the tote board, empty now, except for the names of the contenders.

Just as soon as the polls were closed, people came wandering into the hall. Neatly dressed young people, their faces beaming with excitement, their voices light with laughter. Here again would enter an older man, his brow wrinkled in perpetual worry. There would be the newsmen and reporters too. Occasionally the television

lights would artificially brighten the room
for some short report on how the festivities
were shaping up over at the candidate's
victory party.

So it was on the night of February 26,
1980, that the supporters and volunteers
of Ronald Reagan's presidential campaign
gathered in a Manchester, New Hampshire, motel. This was to be their reward
for the weeks and months of ringing door-
bells, passing out pamphlets and phoning
potential voters. There would be a few
hours of excited anticipation as they await-
ed the results of the balloting. Then would
come tears of joy or sorrow as their hopes
were realized or dreams dashed. If the evening went well, as a special reward they
could count on an appearance by the Governor to thank them for their help.

But there were to be no sorrowful faces
in that Manchester hotel this Tuesday
night. From the time the first reports
began to come across on the television sets,
and their confirmation was written in
chalk on the tote board up front, until the
last styrofoam cup of coffee was emptied
and the last lighted cigarette stubbed out,
it was to be all laughter and cheers.

The room broke into a deafening roar of

yells, whistles and applause. The Governor was making his entrance. The party celebrants climbed on top of chairs and stood on tiptoes, craning their necks to get a better view of their man. Standing on the platform, eyes crinkled in joy, pleasure printed on his face, with one arm raised, hand closed into a fist with thumb extended in a gesture of victory, Ronald Reagan responded to the adulation of his followers. Standing next to him, his arm around her waist, Nancy Reagan, arm raised, hand extended joyfully, shared the moments with the man she loved.

There is no victory so sweet as that snatched from the jaws of defeat. And what a victory it had been. Until the last vote had been cast, the New Hampshire primary had been considered too close to call, but maybe with just a nod in George Bush's direction. The votes had changed it all. Reagan had defeated Bush in a two-to-one landslide; furthermore, he had gained the support of the majority of New Hampshire Republicans, garnering more votes than all the other contenders combined. The final tally: Reagan 50 percent, Bush 23 percent, Baker 13 percent, Anderson 10 percent, Connally and Crane 2 percent each and Bob Dole less than 1/2 percent.

It was a study in contrasts. The sparkling sun, palm trees swaying, a fit, tanned and healthy-looking, casually dressed ex-President Ford standing next to the fatigued, pale and rumpled ex-campaign manager. John Sears had come to Rancho Mirage, and the press was out in full force.

Reports and rumors all seemed to indicate that Gerald Ford was going to jump into the fray. Ford staffers had subtly let slip the names of a series of Midwestern Republican governors who were willing to announce their support for the ex-president. The last possible minute Ford could enter the race and have any chance at victory would be March 21, 1980—the deadline for both the California and Michigan primaries. The rousing victory of Reagan in New Hampshire cast a sense of urgency over a Ford decision. If he didn't move soon, there was the possibility of a rush by the party toward the Californian's bandwagon.

The press, hopefully expecting a Ford announcement naming Sears as a campaign manager, and with it, the former president's entrance into the fray, was disappointed. Instead, Sears and Ford coyly parried thrusts with the reporters beneath the palm trees. No decision, no announcement. Noncandidate Ford was to remain a noncandidate. Ex-campaign manager Sears was to remain an ex-campaign manager, for the time being.

The New Hampshire vote had reestablished Ronald Reagan's status as the front-runner for the Republican nomination. It had also reinforced the impression of an unpredictable and volatile voter's mood. As in Iowa, the polls in New Hampshire could capture only the extreme changes in the voter attitudes and feelings on the various contenders. Reagan was once leading Bush in an early New Hampshire poll by 30 percent, then Bush led Reagan by 10 percent, then it was 50/50, and finally Reagan won by almost 29 percent. 1980 was the year of the unpredictable.

There was no time for rest. March 4 was the date for Massachusetts and Vermont. Bush looked like a big winner in the Bay State. Then there was the southern swing. "Big John" Connally was waiting patiently in South Carolina only four days later on March 8. The reestablished front-runner had his work cut out for him.

The aide rose from his leather chair and polished desk, the press release in his hand. The oak-paneled walls of the outer office of the senior senator from Kansas were lined with photographs. There was a photograph of Robert Dole, arm raised, surrounded by his family receiving the accolades of the 1976 Republican Convention after his acceptance of the vice-presidential nomination. Only 607 New Hampshire Republicans had cast their ballots for Gerald Ford's 1976 running mate. The aide's press release was Robert Dole's statement of impending withdrawal from contention for the 1980 Republican presidential nomination. He promised only to wait until he was on his native Kansas soil to make his announcement formal. The New Hampshire results had drawn the first blood in the Republican race. Robert Dole was the first victim.

6

*Moving Toward
the Showdown*

For over thirty years the ruddy-faced
man with the thinning red hair now laced
in white had come to their factory gates
when he needed the workingman's help.
He was at it once again, stopping each man
who approached the entry post, where the
flash of an I.D. card would gain admit-
tance beyond a little guard station and
inside a chain link fence. Draping an arm
around the worker and softly, in confiden-
tial tones, introducing the tall, silver-haired
man standing with him ("a good man and
great friend of South Carolina") Strom
Thurmond, senior senator from South Carolina, was on the stump with his friend
John Connally. Thurmond was staking his
reputation as the biggest vote getter in

South Carolina on the presidential primary just days away. Since the close of the caucuses in Iowa, while the other candidates had been plowing through New England snows, John Connally, almost always in the company of Senator Thurmond, had been covering South Carolina from the Atlantic Coast to the Appalachian Mountains.

The Connally campaign was placing all of its chips on the table in South Carolina. The big Texan frankly admitted that for him the future of the race would depend upon a first-place finish or close second to Reagan on Saturday, March 8, 1980. Free of federal restrictions on spending, Connally was literally emptying his war chest in laying what he hoped would be a trap for the former California Governor. Over $300,000 had been allocated for this effort. As national attention turned from New Hampshire, it began to look, for all the world, like the Texan might indeed succeed.

The past governor of South Carolina, James Edwards, came out for Connally. Now, the former Texas governor had the state's two most powerful politicians in his camp. The ex-secretary of the treasury did not hesitate to use them. At factory gates, at neighborhood coffees, speaking in small-town squares, the Texan stressed the support local Republican officials were giving him. As the day of voting drew near, Connally, who had not run for an elective office in almost fifteen years, began to warm to his task. The Carolinians were much more receptive to the millionaire oil man than had been the people of Iowa. His speech patterns were not so unfamiliar here in the South. Connally smiled more frequently as his audiences appreciatively listened to his powerful political oratory. His old mastery of the stump began to reassert itself. His confidence, greatly damaged in Iowa, returned. The look of desperation left his eyes. Ronald Reagan would be in for a surprise in South Carolina.

Seven hundred miles to the north, where the stately, colonnaded plantation homes are replaced by the clapboard, cracker box farmhouses just as old, and the cypress draped in Spanish moss is replaced by the strong, bare oak, George Bush, the victor of Iowa, was planning an ambush of his own. The defeat in New Hampshire had thrown the former ambassador for a mo-

mentary loss, but on March 4, Massachusetts and Vermont would be indicating
their preference in the race. George Bush,
a favorite in both places, was determined
to regain momentum.

Massachusetts was the only state to vote
for George McGovern over Richard Nixon
in 1972. Both the Republican and Democratic parties of the state had long liberal
traditions. If ever there was a place alien
to Ronald Reagan's politics, this was it.
Reagan himself realistically admitted his
chances in Massachusetts were slim. The
most prominent of the state's Republicans,
Elliot Richardson and Henry Cabot Lodge,
had already endorsed, and were working
for, Bush. The former ambassador had an
excellent organization in the Bay State
and was spending a good deal of time in
campaign appearances. While the pundits
and pollsters could all predict a Bush win,
the margin of that victory was now very
important to the former ambassador's candidacy. Following Massachusetts and Vermont came a long series of Southern primaries. If John Connally did not stop Reagan
in South Carolina or Bush could not generate a first-place finish in the North large
enough to give him some psychological

help in Florida, the Californian would roll into the crucial Illinois primary like a steam engine. A victory in Illinois for Reagan might well provide a lock on the convention.

The audience was unexpectedly large. The vast majority of the listeners appeared to be young and prosperous. They apparently liked what they heard, for the applause was given often and it was long and loud. The man at the podium looked rather more like a media minister along the order of Robert Schuller than the U.S. congressman from Illinois he was. Trim, well-dressed, distinguished by his white hair and dark, horn-rimmed glasses, John Anderson was delivering his message of clear Republican liberalism to the voters of Massachusetts. Largely ignored by the media, the crowds had been growing in size and enthusiasm. Overlooked by George Bush and forgotten by the Reagan campaign, Anderson was working hard and turning people on.

By the Friday before the primaries, a few local pollsters began to pick up an interesting shift in voter preferences. The name of John Anderson was being repeated with increasing frequency in answer to the question, "Who will you cast your primary vote for?" After the upsets in both Iowa and New Hampshire, the news media did not want to be caught in another surprise, so the schedule of the obscure campaigner from Illinois was checked into. Seemingly all of a sudden on the network Saturday and Sunday newscasts, the nation was treated to reports of a new factor in the Republican race. Coverage of the congressman increased dramatically. By Monday before the Massachusetts and Vermont votes were to be counted, Anderson was being cast as a possible third man in the increasingly two-man race between Reagan and Bush. Cross-party balloting, allowing Democrats to vote in the Republican primary and vice versa had not been a factor in the race up till now, but all of a sudden it was important. Indicators now began to point to a potentially favorable situation for John Anderson.

On Tuesday evening, March 4, 1980, the events of the week began to unfold with a quickening pace. The image beamed into millions of American homes was that of the distinguished and quietly comforting face of anchorman Walter Cronkite. Sitting at his desk, with a huge American flag in red, white and blue, shaped as the United States, behind him, Cronkite announced that once again primary voters had produced a surprise. In a nip-and-tuck race, heavily favored George Bush had just barely edged out the ten-term Illinois congressman John Anderson in Massachusetts. The vote was 124,226 (31.3 percent) for Bush to 123,076 (31 percent) for Anderson. Ronald Reagan had run a surprisingly strong third by capturing 29 percent of the vote. Howard Baker was a distant fourth, garnering only 5 percent of the ballots cast in the Bay State.

The day's other voting in Vermont had produced an equally surprising result with Anderson again coming in a close second. This time it was Reagan who narrowly edged out the Illinois congressman 31 percent to 30 percent. Bush had drawn a disappointing 23 percent of the ballots in Vermont.

Reaction to the results was swift. Bush proclaimed himself delighted to have Anderson, now a major contender, to the left of him and Reagan to the right. But privately, his temper flared again. Anderson, who Bush felt had no real chance at the nomination, had robbed him of an outright victory in the Bay State and kept him from regaining the momentum his campaign now so desperately needed.

Anderson was ecstatic. Pointing to the heavy crossover vote which enabled him to do so well, he proclaimed that, as opposed to Bush and Reagan, he could draw the votes of independents and Democrats as well as Republicans, which would be absolutely essential to capturing the White House in the fall. The showing in the East also brought Anderson the editorial endorsement of two powerful Chicago newspapers, the *Sun-Times* and the *Tribune*. The two papers could play a major role in aiding Anderson in the March 18 Illinois primary, which until the eastern results, figured to be pretty much another Reagan versus Bush battleground. Certainly not the least important factor for Anderson was the overnight increase in campaign contributions and volunteer support as a result of the day's showings.

The Reagan camp, too, was happy. The former California Governor's victory in Vermont had been a mild but pleasant surprise. The vote in Massachusetts was better than expected. But even more important than ballots cast, Reagan had gathered thirteen more delegates in the Bay State. Convention nominations are won by the man with the most delegates and not by the number of primary votes cast. The Reagan campaign had come through the tests in New England with nine more delegates than George Bush, and the southern swing was coming up. If Reagan could hold off the Connally charge in South Carolina he would head into Illinois in a good position to put a cap on the nomination.

On Wednesday, March 5, 1980, the second victim of campaign '80 was claimed. Senator Howard Baker announced his withdrawal from the race by saying, "It was not in the cards." Like Robert Dole who had withdrawn before him, Howard Baker had simply been unable to generate any enthusiasm among the voters. The years of experience in Washington, the devotion to party and party members, even the abilities in campaigning so amply proven in the past, were not enough. 1980 was just not the year for Republican senators seeking the presidential nomination.

By Thursday, March 6, 1980, the rumblings from Rancho Mirage, California, had grown perceptibly louder. The Baker decision had left the old Ford constituency without a candidate; Bush was not really electable. Former secretary of the Air Force and old friend of the former president, Thomas C. Reed, announced the formation of a Draft Ford Committee. Former Secretary of State Henry Kissinger met with Ford and stated he would endorse a Ford candidacy. From New York the state party chairman, Bernard Kilbourn, urged the ex-president to enter the race. The news media picked up and printed a rumor that Stuart Spencer, a prime aide in the 1976 campaign, was putting together a staff once again to make a run for the nomination.

In spite of the vocal support he was arousing, Gerald Ford would have a difficult time of it should he decide to run. Already the deadlines for filing in primaries which would select almost 40 percent of the convention delegates had passed. Ford would have to count on using Baker's name as a surrogate in some of those primaries should Baker prove willing. Entering and winning the remaining primaries for which he still had time to file might look much more difficult from the windows of a campaign bus than from the tinted glass vistas of a mansion on a Rancho Mirage golf course.

Once again, on Saturday night, March 8, 1980, thousands of Americans tuned their television sets to the primary night specials. All day long the Republicans of South Carolina had been responding to the pleas of Ronald Reagan and John Connally at the ballot box. The result was all the Reagan forces could have hoped for. "Big John" Connally's plans of a southern ambush had been shattered. By almost a two-to-one margin, the Republicans of South Carolina had given Ronald Reagan a sweet victory. The tally came out 54 percent, Reagan; 31 percent, Connally; and 15 percent, George Bush. Better still, the Californian had collected all twenty-five of the delegates at stake. John Connally's presidential ambitions lay in a shambles, looking much like one of the abandoned, deteriorating plantation mansions hidden among the moss-covered cypress of the Carolinas.

It was Sunday, March 9, 1980, as the chartered Fairchild F-27, once the airplane of the George Bush Iowa campaign, touched down at the Houston, Texas, airport. Reporters and cameramen crowded toward the Tarmac as the plane taxied into position to unload its passengers. The former governor of Texas, John B. Connally, accompanied by his wife, Nellie, moved toward the anxiously waiting newsmen as the cameras clicked. In a few moments the couple was surrounded by an eager throng of media personnel. Microphones were thrust aggressively toward the distinguished Texan's face. While Nellie Connally reassuringly patted the broad shoulders of her husband's back, John B. Connally, former governor of Texas, former secretary of the navy, former secretary of the treasury, eyes moist and voice quavering, announced to the press corps that he did not intend ever to be a candidate again. (John Connally had spent $11 million and had won only one delegate.) The race for the 1980 Republican presidential nomination had claimed its third victim.

Much later that same day, an exhausted Connally and his wife drove to the exclusive Houston River Oaks Country Club for a late dinner. The couple quietly entered the dimly lit dining room with its oak paneled walls richly decorated in the colors of English racing prints, the candle light glistening off silver, the white tablecloths like ghosts glowing. There was a stir as the Connallys moved through the elegant room toward their table. Heads turned and diners strained to get a glimpse of their famous fellow club members. Then suddenly and quite spontaneously, the handsomely dressed elite of Houston rose from their dinner places and applauded until "Big John" and his wife had been seated.

With John Connally now out of the race, the Reagan bandwagon rolled south through Dixie unimpeded. On March 11, 1980, three southern states held their primaries: Florida, Georgia and Alabama. George Bush had hoped that by gaining a large margin of victory in Massachusetts, coupled with a strong Connally showing in South Carolina, the Bush forces in Florida might turn that primary into a close contest. His wish was not fulfilled. His narrow escape in the Bay State and Reagan's overwhelming triumph in South Carolina had pushed Florida, once considered the Californian's weakest point in the South, solidly into the former Governor's column. The results in

the most politically moderate of the southern states gave Reagan 57 percent of the
vote and fifty-one delegates to Bush's 30
percent of the vote and no delegates. John
Anderson, who had made no appearances
in the South and had no organization
there, managed to gather 10 percent of
Florida's Republican ballots.

The Florida story was repeated, but
with greater emphasis, in Georgia. In
President Carter's home state, Ronald
Reagan once again captured all the delegates at stake, thirty-six, and rolled up a
whopping 76 percent of the vote to Bush's
mere 13 percent. Here too, however, a
specter of the importance of the coming
showdown in Illinois reared its head. John
Anderson, again with no organization or
campaigning, scored 10 percent of the
vote.

In Alabama almost four times the number of Republicans who voted in the 1976
primary turned out to give 73 percent of
their votes to Ronald Reagan. Bush only
managed to capture 26 percent of the ballots cast in this, the most southern state.
Tuesday, March 11, 1980, had been a very
good day for the presidential fortunes of
Ronald Wilson Reagan.

The rains of mid-March bring with them the promise of spring to come in Washington, D.C. They wash away the last residue of the winter's snows, by now encrusted with a black layer of soot. The cherry trees along the basin sprout green again, and the earliest of the spring flowers begin to lift their heads above the soil in the city's myriad parks and little squares. It was to this city, freshening itself after the long winter's siege, that Gerald Ford, former president of the United States, called together the men who would be responsible for his campaign should he decide to run once again for the presidency. These strategists and campaign experts were to analyze the possible scenarios which would give Ford the Republican party's convention once again. The former president had delayed his decision to the last possible minute. He had to make his mind up now. Along with the campaign organizers and professionals, Ford had issued an invitation to eighteen Republican governors to join the Washington meeting. Only four had responded positively; the governor's assembly was canceled.

Returning by jet to the warmth of the desert sun, Gerald Ford announced a press conference for late that same week. His mind was made up. Standing outside his home in Rancho Mirage, the former president faced the gathered members of the media. Only a week before, a smiling Jerry Ford had stood under the same palm trees, his former secretary of state, Henry Kissinger, by his side, telling the press how he had urged his old boss to enter the fray. Just a week before that, John Sears, Ronald Reagan's former political engineer, had stood with the smiling ex-president and parried thrusts with the press.

This time, however, Ford stood alone and spoke in measured tones to the bank of microphones before him. He had reached a final and certain decision, the toughest of his life. "Our country is in very deep trouble," he said. "America needs a new president." But he went on to say that he was out of the race. Ford did not want to divide his party. He would not become a candidate and would support the party nominee with all the energy he had. It was over; the contender who never officially entered had quit. It seemed that in spite of the vocal assurances of many, too few were actually willing to join battle on his side.

And so it came to be that the Reagan

Convention Express, after a slow start in Iowa, roared into Illinois very much according to schedule. On board were 202 of the 998 delegates necessary to capture the 1980 Republican presidential nomination. But more importantly, the "Big Mo," as George Bush had called it, was now riding the Reagan bandwagon.

7

The Final Showdown

A babble of excited voices filled the air. Every chair in the ballroom of Chicago's Continental Plaza Hotel was taken; the occupants were engaged in animated conversation. Distinguished-looking middle-aged businessmen and university students dressed in tee shirts and blue jeans discussed how Ronald Reagan might attack John Anderson's stand on a fifty-cent gasoline tax. Matronly ladies with blue-tinted gray hair clutched their Gucci bags as they argued the merits of Philip Crane with former anti-war activists who were now prosperous suburbanite mothers draped in designer dresses, with their hair coifed in the latest West Coast fashions.

Standing in the back of the elegant hall,

gathered in little clusters, stood the clean-scrubbed, neatly attired, handsome aides of the four men who would meet shortly on the stage. The youthful group of Anderson supporters basked in the glow of reflected glory, beaming confidence, speaking little; one or another nodding now and then at a member of the media. These were new-found friends who had flocked together after the upsets in Massachusetts and Vermont. The directive from Anderson himself was to treat them right.

The Bush group, with anxiety written on their brows, talked quietly among themselves. Their faces were almost prayerful in attitude as they hoped their man would avoid another disaster like the second New Hampshire debate. One or two of them could be seen glancing enviously at the Anderson entourage, which was so obviously enjoying the attention the media was giving to their new star. That attention had once belonged to them; it must be won back if the ex-director of the CIA was going to stop Reagan.

Smallest of all was the collection of Phil Crane's few volunteers. They clustered in a defensive huddle, briefly exchanging a word here or there with a recognizable supporter seated in the audience. It was not fair, it seemed to them, that Anderson should be drawing so much attention while their man was being ignored. Crane was an Illinois congressman also, but the big Chicago papers had endorsed John Anderson while all but ignoring Crane, the other "home state boy" in the race.

Then there was the group of Reagan men. They were gamely recognizing people in the audience or among the media personnel but they still seemed worried just the same. Their stony faces reflected the pain of having been excluded—not excluded from the excitement of the event or the campaign, but excluded from the inner circle that was gathered in a side room with the Governor. If they were outside in Chicago, would they be outside when their man eventually won the White House? They were all confident Ronald Reagan would win the nomination and the election; when that happened, influence on the hard trail of the primaries would be translated into power in Washington.

The media scurried throughout the room. A soundman bustled up to the platform to check the audio pickup. The television director, with his headset on, trailed a cord behind him while speaking into his little microphone, suggesting new camera angles or lighting requirements. The cameramen and assistants were busy wheeling around their magic eyes, with cables unrolling behind them to some distant location out of the room where a moment in Chicago would soon be translated into a picture in Los Angeles or New York. These professionals, who had done this same job before in New Hampshire, Iowa, or South Carolina, added to the electrically charged atmosphere of anticipation in the ballroom. No one was immune to the feeling.

Everyone—spectators, aides, media personnel—knew the forum tonight would be different from the earlier debates. This would be a showdown; the Illinois primary was at stake. Tonight could make or break any of the four contenders. Dole, Baker and Connally, participants in the earlier confrontations, were out of the race. Clearly, Crane, Bush, Anderson, and Reagan were now more interested in establishing their political differences than in maintaining the camaraderie of the previous forums. The debate in Chicago would give the contenders the chance to point out those variations in beliefs.

The bright lights flashed on, bathing the ballroom stage in a harsh white; at the same instant, the sea of voices rose to a climactic, fevered pitch of anticipation and then fell silent. The hush in the ballroom was charged with excitement. With the solemnity of an ecclesiastical procession, Philip Crane, George Bush, Ronald Reagan and John Anderson filed onto the platform with the moderator, Howard K. Smith.

All semblance of religious ceremony was quickly removed from the evening's proceedings as soon as the five men were seated. A large blue-and-white banner proclaimed, "League of Women Voters 1980 Presidential Forum." With amazing speed, Philip Crane lashed out at his congressional colleague, John Anderson. George Bush, in a manner only slightly more reserved than Crane's, joined in the criticism of the momentarily nonplussed Anderson. Howard K. Smith appeared befuddled in his attempts to conduct the forum, now totally different from the previous two debates which had been so reserved. Only Ronald Reagan remained aloof from the fracas.

Crane angrily accused Anderson of supporting Democratic candidates for reelection. He further denounced Anderson as being a traitor to the Republican Party. Meanwhile, the former California Governor was sitting silently. George Bush rapped Anderson's stand on Social Security so repeatedly that at one point Anderson, with his voice quavering in indignation, interrupted a Bush monologue. In forceful tones Anderson declared, "That is just not so, Mr. Bush."

The blatant animosity of Crane and Bush toward Anderson served to underscore the dignity of Ronald Reagan. Responding firmly and quietly, only to the questions asked of him, the Californian remained benignly above the arguments. During the months prior to Iowa, John Sears had tried to portray his candidate, Ronald Reagan, as presidential material, a cut above the crowded field of contenders, by devising a strategy which called for limited public appearances and no debating. It had not worked. In the Chicago debate Reagan's thoughtful answers and dignified demeanor succeeded in conveying the very impression Sears' winter strategy had tried so hard to do.

The former Governor relaxed with his

eyes twinkling and a trace of a smile on his face. He watched in bemused silence while his opponents struck out at one another with biting sarcasm, more like political machine ward healers than the presidential contenders they claimed to be.

In Iowa, Reagan had clearly lost because he had not participated in the forum. In the first New Hampshire debate, he had capped the lid over a potential problem through an open and honest answer to a tough question. South Carolina's debate had given nothing nor taken anything away. The Illinois confrontation served to underscore Reagan's ability to act and look like a president. The Republican front-runner had faced his challengers as no other presidential hopeful before him ever had, and he came through with his colors flying high. When the showdown in Chicago was over and the dust had settled, only Ronald Reagan came through unscathed.

Regardless of the show at Chicago's Continental Plaza Hotel, it was John Anderson who was reading the newspaper polls with delight. A *Chicago Sun-Times* survey, conducted throughout the state, indicated

Anderson was leading Reagan by a nose as the favorite of Illinois Republicans for the party's nomination. That prediction was confirmed by yet another state-wide poll. The crowds at the Anderson rallies were huge and enthusiastic. Campaign contributions were rolling into Anderson headquarters at the rate of $150,000 a day, compared to only $456,000 for all of 1979. Financially, the Illinois congressman was sitting in an enviable position. Because of his early lack of funds, Anderson had not been able to spend as freely as Bush or Reagan in the first primaries, but, with the new money coming in, he would be able to outmatch his rivals in the crucial contests of Wisconsin, Ohio and Michigan, which followed Illinois. Reagan and Bush had both come perilously close to their legal spending limits. John Anderson had much further to go before reaching his.

The picture was now becoming familiar to Americans everywhere. With snowy hair, thin and distinguished face, horn-rimmed glasses, and outspread arms, John Anderson beckoned for the votes of Democrats and Independents. He proclaimed his message across the plains of Illinois with enthusiastic fervor. Reporters, commentators, television correspondents, soundmen and cameramen recorded Anderson's every word and move as if they were seeking forgiveness for the months they had ignored "John Who?" It was heady stuff for a once-obscure candidate. Just as George Bush had been before him, John Anderson now became the darling of the media. Where Bush had responded to the attention with ecstatic enthusiasm, Anderson responded with the high-brow zeal of an academic crusader.

While the Anderson campaign was sweeping through Illinois like a prairie fire, the Reagan forces were doing their work as thoroughly as a combine harvests wheat. Quietly, and with the dignity which had been so evident in the Chicago debate, Ronald Reagan appealed to the Republicans of Illinois. There appeared to be a new sense of purpose in the Californian. The frantic, hectic atmosphere of the New Hampshire campaign seemed to have yielded to a steadier, more secure and confident feeling. Perhaps this change in attitude was the result of the withdrawals of Dole, Baker and Connally and the removal of Ford as a potential rival. Perhaps it was the result of being in the Midwest—Illinois was, after all, the Californian's original home. Whatever the reason, the result was a relaxed, confident Reagan. Schedules, however, were no easier. There were still the chicken dinners, the rallies in high-school auditoriums, the parades.

In Ronald Reagan's home town, banners stretched across Main Street: "Welcome Home, Governor Reagan"; "Galesburg for Reagan"; "Reagan for President." A motor-cade, headed proudly by Galesburg's two lime-green fire engines, moved patiently down the street, lined on both sides by farmers, merchants, professionals—all the people who make a small community work. Smiling broadly, waving, nodding recog-nition here and there, the little town's most famous former grade-school student slowly rolled past many of his old classmates, their children and grandchildren. Ronald Reagan had come once again to Galesburg. There are few moments so pleasurable to the campaigning politician as the warm and boisterous welcome of an old home town. They were proud of him, those peo-ple lining the streets. He could feel it. It was but a brief moment, but it was a moment that made the harder ones endurable. Illinois had not yet forgotten that Ronald Reagan once lived there. Maybe on Tuesday the voters would remember too.

"J.B.A., J.B.A., J.B.A.!" The chant filled the Chicago ballroom. It was Tuesday night, March 18, 1980. The supporters of John Anderson had gathered for a victory celebration. The smoke-filled room was jammed to the walls with happy, cheering people, their bright faces cleansed by an ordeal now finished and their fatigue momentarily replaced with the joyful emotion of a job completed.

"J.B.A., J.B.A!" The chant continued. The balloting had now ceased. The results were in: Ronald Reagan, not John Anderson, had been swept to victory in the Illinois Republican primary. The campaign tote board off to the side of the platform had chalked the news—the former California Governor had 48 percent of the vote and a resounding victory. Still, the crowded ballroom echoed with the chant, "J.B.A., J.B.A!"

Finally, he appeared to a roar of approval. J.B.A. had lost the primary. His second-place finish was not even close—37 percent. But that information on the board up front did not matter to those gathered that night. "Politics," he said, "means more than just a game of winning and losing. It is instead a chance for an honest effort to chart a new course for the nation." John Anderson, to the chants and cheers of 1,800 enthusiastic followers, was claiming moral victory. After telling the packed ballroom that the old ideas and old politics will not do any more, Anderson broke into a smile and led the room filled with backers in a rousing chorus of "On, Wisconsin," the fight song of the University of Wisconsin. Wisconsin was to be the next major battleground.

Moral victory clear or not, the ballots had firmly declared Ronald Reagan the favorite presidential contender in Illinois. The primary gave him forty-one more convention delegates. Anderson's appeal to Independents and Democrats to cross over and vote in the Republican primary had produced an uncounted-on result. While the vast majority of these crossovers cast their ballots for the Illinois congressman, fully a third placed their marks in Reagan's column. The victory gave the Californian an almost certain nomination at the Republicans' Detroit convention. The win in a large industrial state of the Midwest, after the scores in both the Northeast and South, removed from the former Governor the stigma of an appeal based only on geographic or philosophical lines. The denial of first place for Anderson in his home state, in spite of the claims of moral victory, took the wind from the congressman's sails. Bush, whose efforts drew a mere 11 percent and garnered only two delegates, dropped further back. John Anderson, George Bush, or Philip Crane would not be able to stop the Reagan bandwagon. It was too far ahead and pulling even farther away.

The next week, on March 28, Reagan came within a whisker of stealing a victory from George Bush in Bush's childhood home state of Connecticut. The same day in New York's primary, where the voters cast ballots for the actual delegates rather than the contenders, the Californian won an astounding 105 of the state's 123 representatives to the convention. John Connally, the former contender, announced his support for Reagan. The media, sensing now a Reagan-Carter conflict in the fall, began to turn its attention toward the issues which separated the two front-runners and the findings of national polls, which were showing Reagan to be gaining on the President in popularity.

On April 1, 1980, the chalkboards in the campaign headquarters showed Reagan had ended any possibility John Anderson might have had for the nomination by beating both him and George Bush in the Wisconsin primary. As returns were phoned in to the storefront offices of the Anderson and Bush forces, sad-eyed aides with chalk-powdered hands would once again erase the figures. Each time, the number next to Reagan's name increased until the final tally was posted late in the evening: Reagan—40 percent; Bush—31 percent; Anderson—28 percent. There was little chance now that Reagan could be denied the nomination, even if by some remote chance the party desired to do so. The first round of primaries had finished. The Californian held 345 committed delegates, compared to Bush's 72 and Anderson's 57.

On April 17, 1980, the congressional office of Philip Crane issued a press release announcing that the Illinois congressman was withdrawing from the race. The youngest man in the contest had failed to light any fires. His boyish good looks had been more than offset by his acerbic demands for conservative purity. Nonetheless, the congressman had brought national recognition to himself. While his withdrawal drew even less attention from the press than had his early entry into the contest, it was certain the young man would be heard from again—perhaps, even yet in 1980 as a vice-presidential nominee.

The seemingly endless round of primaries began again on April 22 in Pennsylvania. The picture carried in newspapers across the country the next day showed a smiling George Bush, with his arm upraised, hair tousled, suit coat open, and his tie blowing in the wind. His wife, Barbara, was at his side with the pleasure of victory written upon her features. But the sparkle had left the former ambassador's eyes. The buoyant, even boisterous Bush of the Iowa-to-New Hampshire Indian Summer was gone. Even the victory in Pennsylvania could not hide the numbing fatigue of fighting a losing battle. It had cost the ex-director of the CIA fourteen days of time and one million dollars to defeat

Reagan in the Keystone State. The vote was 54 percent for Bush, 45 percent for the Californian. But in the more crucial delegate count, the Governor had gained thirty-three votes for the Detroit convention to Bush's seventeen.

Two days after the Pennsylvania results, John Anderson made a major announcement. Standing before the impersonal eye of television cameras, the fifty-six-year-old congressman from Rockford, Illinois, told his watching audience that he would henceforth seek the presidency as an independent candidate. The statement was not totally unexpected—for the past month a number of prominent Anderson supporters had been urging him to go the route of being Independent. The 1980 Republican nominating process had claimed its fifth victim. Only two candidates remained in the Republican race: Reagan and Bush.

The road was truly clear for the California Governor. By Tuesday, May 6, 1980, he had accumulated 746 of the 998 delegates necessary to win the nomination. There was no question of what the outcome in Detroit would be. Bush was capable of a surprise here and there, the Texas primary was closer than expected, yet Reagan had won sixty-one of the eighty delegates.

Tuesday evening, May 20, 1980, George Bush, his wife, Barbara, his sons, and a few trusted aides gathered in a hotel room to watch the returns from the Michigan primary on television. There had been little in the way of good news for the Bush forces since the Pennsylvania upset two weeks before. The outcome this evening was crucial. If the ex-director of the CIA was to continue challenging Reagan, he had to win in Michigan.

The picture captured that evening was in stark contrast to that taken so many weeks ago in New Hampshire. This time, the candidate was seen with pleasure stamped over the lines of fatigue etched on his handsome face; his wife was beaming with joy at this vindication of her man; his aides and his sons, with their eyes gleaming in victory and revenge, were rushing from the room to return with the figures verifying the victory. He had won, and he had won big: 58 percent Bush, 32 percent Reagan. The race was still on.

The supporters' victory celebration in Detroit that evening was conducted with all the frenzied abandon of a good thing that had been denied too long. The cheers and yells were louder, the applause longer, the cigarette smoke thicker than any had ever been at the few previous winner's celebrations the Bush campaign had enjoyed. It was an exhausted, but happy George Bush who retired to bed on the night of May 20, 1980.

With eager anticipation, the former ambassador's aides rose early to see how the press had responded to their boss's overwhelming victory the day before. The first headlines were viewed in shocked disbelief. The joy of Tuesday night was quickly erased. Papers in hand, the aides hurried back to their hotel rooms and switched on the networks' early morning shows to confirm what they had read. It was true. In spite of the Michigan victory, the TV networks had projected Ronald Reagan to be the Republican presidential nominee. With delegates already committed to vote for the Californian, plus others who were noncommitted but indicating they would cast their ballots for Reagan, the former Governor had the number necessary to win the nomination on the first ballot. It was a bitter blow.

Solemnly the news was broken to George Bush. A hurried staff conference followed.

A press release was issued, announcing
the former ambassador would cancel all
campaign appearances, return home, and
review his bid for the nomination.

Four hundred supporters and a phalanx
of media corpsmen gathered in the ballroom of the Houston Marriott Hotel on
Monday, May 26, 1980. George Bush was
to make an announcement. For five days
he and his staff had been ensconced in the
ambassador's palatial Houston home, analyzing facts and figures, deciding on the
course to follow in light of network projec-
tions. In the glow of television lights,
standing beside his wife and before a room
of wildly cheering supporters, George Bush,
after two years of campaigning at a cost of
$16.2 million, announced, "There is a wide-
spread perception that the campaign is
over. As a result, it has become increasingly difficult to raise the funds needed.
My overwhelming instinct was to stay and
fight . . . but you've got to be realistic."
Bush went on to throw his "wholehearted
support" to Ronald Reagan and released
his delegates, urging them to vote for the
Californian at the Detroit convention.

The pundits and press could now turn

their attention to differences between the three candidates for the presidency— Reagan, the Republican; Carter, the Democrat; and Anderson, the Independent. The race for the nomination was over. It had been, in many ways, a totally unpredictable contest. The voters' moods had been volatile and not easily measured by usually reliable pollsters. But in spite of it all, the early front-runner had finished ahead, and, except for the unknowable factor of John Anderson, the final combatants were the same men who had been predicted almost a year before.

November 13, 1979. Ronald Reagan announces for the presidency.

Reagan greets factory workers.

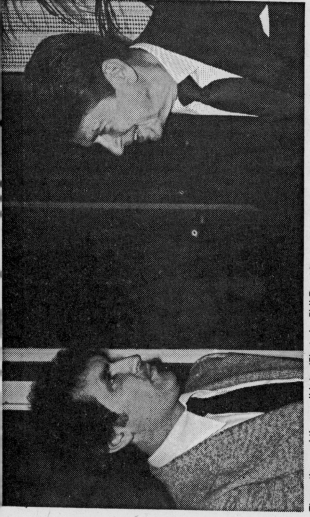

The author and the candidate. (Photo by Phil Egert.)

143

George Otis and the Governor preparing for the interview. (Photo by High Adventure Ministries.)

They met on a blind date, Ron and Nancy Reagan. (Photo by Roger Sandler.)

With North Carolina kingmaker, Dexter Yager, and his wife, Birdie. (Photo by Bill Childers.)

With friends, Bill and Peggy Britt. (Photo by Tony Renard.)

Author, Doug Wead; former congressman and Reagan religious liaison, John Conlan; the Rev. Mr. Cecil Todd; and entertainer Pat Boone at a Reagan Dinner. (Photo by Phil Egert.)

The candidate aboard chartered plane during announcement trip. (Photo by Roger Sandler.)

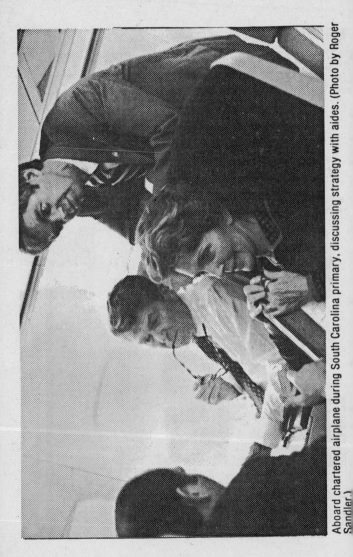

Aboard chartered airplane during South Carolina primary, discussing strategy with aides. (Photo by Roger Sandler.)

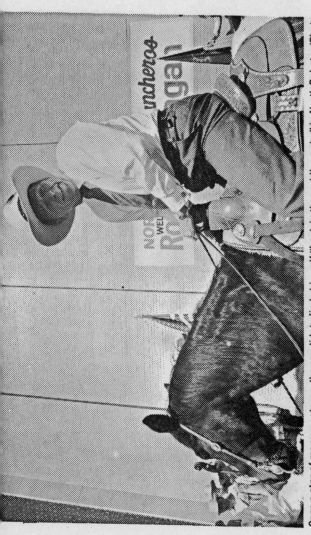

Once a star of many westerns, the candidate finds himself "back in the saddle again," in North Dakota. (Photo by Roger Sandler.)

A genuine Midwestern welcome. (Photo by Roger Sandler.)

Hard at work in his Los Angeles office. (Photo by Roger Sandler.)

Ronald Reagan with his family at Announcement Night dinner in New York City. From left to right: Ronald Reagan, Maureen Reagan, Nancy Reagan, Patti Reagan, Michael Reagan and his wife, and Ronnie Reagan.

(Photo by Roger Sandler.)

154

Barbara Walters interviews the candidate. (Photo by Roger Sandler.)

With deep concern for America, Ronald Reagan ponders the future.
(Photo by Roger Sandler.)

Epilog

Reagan and his wife, Nancy, entered the Charlotte, North Carolina, Colosseum with a massive entourage of campaign aides, Secret Service men and reporters. They were led through a cordon of admirers, and into a holding room offstage.

Some of the campaign staff had preceded them. Former Congressman John Conlan, appearing in the city the day before, had warned a group of businessmen that they were really needed now to make meaningful campaign contributions. He netted $35,000 as a result. Conlan would be going to an important rendezvous with evangelist Billy Graham the next day but not before introducing the Governor to some of his new contributors.

They formed a line in the holding room, handsome men in dark suits and beautiful ladies with dazzling earrings and floor-length dresses. "Governor, this is Mr. and Mrs. Jerry Meadows, two of your key supporters."

"Yes, good to see you," Reagan would smile and extend his hand and Nancy would sometimes give the wife a little hug. There would be a series of popping flash-bulbs and then the line would move up once more.

"Governor, this is Mr. and Mrs. Rex Renfro. . . ."

I watched the repetitious scene for a few minutes and then wandered out into the hall, behind the chairman of the event, Dexter Yager. One of the South's leading businessmen, Yager had a reputation for financing patriotic causes and was rumored to be among the top ten money raisers for the Reagan Primary Campaign.

Yager grabbed me and pulled me close, "What's the word on the vice president?" He had to shout to keep his voice above the crowd. "Who do you think Reagan is going to go with?"

"They are talking about Richard Lugar," I said.

Yager smiled, nodding towards the massive audience of 15,000 Americans. "Remember the first time Reagan spoke to my people?" There was a little twinkle in his eye. It was in 1976 and the newspapers had credited Yager's last-minute massive rally and brigades of campaign workers for stealing the Republican primary from Gerald Ford. It was Reagan's first primary victory of 1976 and, though a late beginning, he had taken the nomination from an incumbent president.

"You are going to get up there and speak next," Yager ordered. "My people don't know I have Reagan on the program. Secret Service rules. I couldn't advertise it." He jabbed his stubby finger in my stomach, "I want you to do a good job introducing the Governor."

I wandered around the back of the colosseum for a few moments trying to get something organized for the introduction. There was not much time, but as luck would have it, the audience was much too distracted to hear me anyway. The television networks had begun to set up their own makeshift stage, and bright lights suddenly washed the scene. Secret Service men began fanning out into the aisles.

The audience caught on to my not-too-subtle hint and started going wild. By the time Ronald and Nancy Reagan were on stage, the 15,000 people were on their feet with a deafening roar of welcome. The greeting was so long and so enthusiastic that it temporarily threw the Governor's timing off.

He started into the first line of his speech but it did not work. This audience already knew what he would probably say and they were not finished letting him know they agreed. He smiled patiently, tried to calm the cheers and then turned sheepishly to Nancy who was seated behind him. These people just would not quiet down.

Reagan finally gave in, bathing self-consciously in the applause, knowing these were people who viewed the world the same way he did and they were happy to see him winning. Their views were prevailing. They were essentially applauding themselves.

It was a moving speech, not eloquent or profound by Reagan's own standards, but an incredible demonstration of how to handle a cumbersome, wild and sympathetic audience. His words were interrupted frequently by rounds of tremendous applause.

During one awkward moment, some sympathetic people began to sing "God Bless America" right in the middle of his speech. Reagan paused for a minute to see if his enthusiastic audience wanted to sing, and then he moved on to other peaks and crescendos.

The most dramatic moment came when Reagan told a story that illustrated the difference between "our free society and a totalitarian one."

In Reagan's tale, the Soviet Union awards its highest medal to the assassin of Leon Trotsky. The United States gave hers "to a different kind of man, a man on a plane which had been fatally damaged and was falling from the sky. The crew was preparing to bail out when they heard cries from the fuselage. A wounded gunner was trapped by the twisted metal.

"The boy wailed in panic, 'Don't leave me!'

"America's medal of honor was posthumously awarded to one of the brave air force commanders. He had ordered his men to parachute to safety but he himself had stayed on board choosing to lose his life to provide a little comfort to a dying American serviceman."

This story was told with great skill, but the warmth and response of the audience almost overwhelmed the speaker. Reagan stood as the crowd cheered and shouted. His eyes were moist and for one brief moment he and the audience were transfixed, locked in a case of mutual admiration.

Like the union blue-collar workers who had crossed over from the Democratic Party to vote for Reagan in the primaries, like the Jews who had supported him for his life-long, sympathetic support of Israel, like the Christians who stood with him for morality, these were his people. In fact, they could claim to be the original Reagan voting block, his base of support. They were the so-called middle Americans, the silent majority.

"I do not agree with those who say that our country must now decline, that we have no choice but to fail," Reagan told them. "I believe in the American Dream!"

And they cheered—young men in dark blue suits, and young ladies with bright faces. They cheered. I looked out over the thousands of people and in that moment, I remembered one of the Governor's famous lines, "There never has been a silent majority, the problem is that a lot of people in government have been deaf!"

The thunderous roar of applause hung over the stage long after the candidate and his wife had evacuated the building and begun their limousine drive to the airport. None could doubt, the silent majority had spoken in North Carolina that day, and no one could doubt they would be heard from again—all across America.

Ronald Reagan-George Otis Interview

George Otis of High Adventure Ministries in Van Nuys, California, conducted an exclusive interview with Ronald Reagan. Mr. Otis asked Governor Reagan a number of questions never before presented to any presidential candidate.

This interview was incorporated in the High Adventure television series, which regularly has as guests Christian newsmakers and celebrities.

George Otis is an active lay Christian speaker and author. We gratefully acknowledge his permission to reprint this intriguing interview.

George Otis: This interview with Governor Ronald Reagan is a historic first, and I trust it will set a tradition in America that we will take time with every candidate who presents himself for a major position of leadership in this nation to learn his views concerning moral and spiritual issues.

Governor Reagan, it is a privilege to talk

to you, and I would like to just ask you a few questions. On so many of the great issues today we almost seem to be extolling compromise, pragmatism and accommodation. It is so often situation ethics and situational morals which seem to be guiding forces in our society today. I would like to know if you think that principles and absolutes are really becoming obsolete.

Ronald Reagan: Well, I think there has been a great tendency that way. Yes, I think there has been a wave of humanism or hedonism throughout the land. It has happened before in history, and I think we have experienced it. . . . Our educators, for instance, want to do away with *in loco parentis.* They no longer want a responsibility for anything other than the classroom with regard to the students who come to the colleges in the land. This has spread to lower levels of education to where the moral ethic is supposedly not the function of education. And, in the situational ethic, . . . there are some who say, "Well there are no absolutes." I, however, am optimistic because I sense in this land a great revolution against that. A feeling of unhappiness, or anchorlessness,

I think is responsible for much of what has happened to our youth, because they feel without guidelines that they are without an anchor.

George Otis: What you are sensing, then, as you travel back and forth across the United States is a change in our moral commitments?

Ronald Reagan: Oh, I think there is a hunger in this land for a spiritual revival. A return to a belief in moral absolutes. The same morals upon which the nation was founded.

George Otis: The great historian, Arnold Toynbee, said, "Unless there be a great spiritual renewal there is no hope for this earth." So it is kind of important today.

Ronald Reagan: That's right.

George Otis: God says, "I am the same today, yesterday and forever," so His thoughts are the same and don't necessarily change to fit contemporary circumstances. Do you believe that is correct?

Ronald Reagan: Yes. They say that in his entire history man has written about four billion laws and with all the four billion they haven't improved on the Ten Commandments one bit.

George Otis: That certainly is a profound statement. You know, I have a copy of a statement you made during the Bicentennial regarding a need for spiritual renewal in America, and I wonder if I could impose upon you to share it. Would you mind reading it to us so we might know just what you feel?

Ronald Reagan: Yes, I remember when this was asked of me, and it wasn't easy to boil it down to a few paragraphs or one page, but the best I could do was to say: "In this Bicentennial year we are daily reminded that our strength and our greatness grew from a national commitment to God and country. Those institutions of freedom which became famous worldwide were forged in the fires of spiritual belief; yet today many of these institutions are in jeopardy.

"The time has come to turn back to God and reassert our trust in Him for the healing of America. This means that all of us who acknowledge a belief in our Judeo-Christian heritage must reaffirm that belief and join forces to reclaim those great principles embodied in that Judeo-Christian tradition and in ancient Scripture. Without such a joining of forces, the materialist *quantity* of life in our country may increase for a time, but the *quality* of life will continue to decrease.

"As a Christian I commit myself to do my share in this joint venture.

"Our Country is in need of and ready for a spiritual renewal. Such a renewal is based on spiritual reconciliation—man with God, and then man with man. . . . One lesson should be that as a nation it's 'In God We Trust.' "

George Otis: That is pretty straight talk. God sent a "telegram" to this country, and I think it might be responsible for some of the good changes you are talking about and are interested in bringing to pass on an escalated basis. It is something you said before that is just ricocheting across the land, a statement taken from 2 Chronicles 7:14 which is very much like what you are saying now: "If my people, which are called by my name, shall humble themselves, and pray, and seek my face, and turn from their wicked ways; then will I hear from heaven, and will forgive their sin, and will heal their land."

Ronald Reagan: There is one thing about campaigning. We talk about how hard it is, but when you go out across the country and meet the people, you can't help but pray and remind God of that passage in 2 Chronicles, because the people of this country are not beyond redemption. They are good people and I believe this nation has a destiny as yet unfulfilled.

George Otis: It is really encouraging to hear you say that. This is what Aleksandr Solzhenitsyn is speaking. There is a need to believe that God will heal our land, and He works very much through people.

I would like to get your views on the separation of church and state. We know that is an important constitutional principle in this country. Does this mean God should be divorced from public affairs? Does it mean that Christians shouldn't be involved in the political arena?

Ronald Reagan: No. There is a widespread interpretation in many areas that separation of church and state means separation from God. The early Americans had seen what happened when church attempted to dictate to state—or when state attempted to dictate to church—and I think this is all that it meant. This concept is based on the idea that I think is inherent in Jesus' teachings, and that every man must find salvation for himself and for his own soul. And, therefore, there should be no official interference in this.

George Otis: Somebody has said that separation of church and state simply means that religious organizations should not run the government and that the government should not run the religious organizations. Do you subscribe to that?

Ronald Reagan: I think that is all it means, and the steps that have been taken in recent years, supposedly under a threat of violation of church and state in this country, I don't think have been based on *ever* there being a clear and present danger of this happening.

George Otis: What are your views on legislating prayer out of the school? It is really legislating God out of the schools in a way. How do you feel about that?

Ronald Reagan: I don't think He ever should have been expelled! First of all, there is a double threat there. . . . Those who didn't feel they should (pray), all right, it is their right to remain silent. But the second threat is that by taking prayer out it appears in the eyes of young people that there has been an official ruling out of God—that, therefore, He isn't of sufficient importance to be in the schools.

George Otis: That is pretty serious stuff, isn't it?

Ronald Reagan: Yes, it is.

George Otis: Now I want to ask you a very personal question. You have said and written in your spiritual statement that you are a Christian. I would like to know what that means to you. In the New Testament it tells about a Jewish leader who came one night to Jesus and asked Jesus about His relationship with God. Jesus answered back to him, "Except a man be born again, he cannot see the kingdom of God." Chuck Colson, the Nixon lawyer who went to prison, used that very phrase, "born again," as the title of his book. It is the story of his conversion and the changes in his own life, and I would like to know what this phrase "born again" means to you. And, if it is not too personal, have you been born again?

Ronald Reagan: Well, I think I know what

the expression means. I certainly know what the meaning of it is today among those who believe in it. I can't remember a time in my life when I didn't call upon God and hopefully thank Him as often as I called upon Him. And yes, in my own experience there came a time when there developed a new relationship with God, and it grew out of need. So, yes, I have had an experience that could be described as "born again."

George Otis: That is very interesting. It was a very straight statement that Jesus made to Nicodemus. And you are saying, "Yes, I have really answered back to Jesus and said I want you to be the leader of my life. I want God to be my leader." Is that what you are saying?

Ronald Reagan: That is what I am saying.

George Otis: You know another thing on the moral line is that millions today are troubled about the avalanche of pornography and sexual vice. Things like murder, rape, broken homes and child abuse seem to be increasing greatly. We would like to know if you personally see any hope of a reversal of this moral pollution.

Ronald Reagan: Oh, yes. It isn't too easy to see now, but I believe the tide has turned. I think that the hunger I mentioned earlier has become evident. I think the contrast of their (young people's) attitude today with a few years ago reveals this hunger. These problems won't be solved by some sudden sweeping over the land of a warning or something. It is going to come from within the people themselves. I think they are already feeling it.

George Otis: This spiritual revolution we have been talking about is a wave of people being born again and becoming conscious of God. Do you think this may be just a product of it?

Ronald Reagan: Yes.

George Otis: Is this where our hope lies?

Ronald Reagan: Yes, yes.

George Otis: The legislature of the state you governed for a couple of terms has recently passed a law which legalizes adults practicing homosexuality and sadism. I would like to ask you a pointed question. If this sodomy bill had reached your desk while you were still in office, would you have signed it?

Ronald Reagan: No. I would have vetoed it. I know there is a quarrel here with so many very fine people who have a libertarian approach to government. They believe in more individual freedom. So some of these people would quarrel with this, because they would carry libertarianism all the way to whatever an individual wanted to do. But I have always believed that the body of man-made law must be founded upon the higher natural law. You can make immorality legal but you cannot make it moral.

George Otis: That's intensely basic to what we are talking bout here, and the Bible talks about a time when everybody did "what seemed good in their sight." It produced a horrible condition upon the earth. It brought on murder, violence and that sort of thing. What you are saying here is that we really cannot stand for spiritual, moral anarchy and have a peaceful place to live.

Ronald Reagan: That is right.

George Otis: Many have been concerned about the increase of drug- and alcohol-related problems in America. It is really a growing concern. Even so, several state legislatures are now lifting legal restraints and thereby moral restraints, I feel, on marijuana. Some are now saying this drug should be legitimized at the federal level. Do you advocate the legalizing of marijuana?

Ronald Reagan: No. I was opposed to it all the time I was governor. I still am opposed to it. First of all, I think that it is a far more dangerous drug than most people are prepared to admit. I speak from some knowledge, because I had to learn a great deal about it when I was governor, and it is probably one of the greatest threats confronting young Americans. The second thing is this: If the government takes the marijuana-legalizing position, once again you have almost put an official seal of approval on this drug. This means we have said to a generation of young people, "Well, we don't take it very seriously. We don't think it is so harmful after all." No, I wish . . . that a generation of young Americans would decide they would be the generation that doesn't need a crutch.

George Otis: You know, Governor Reagan, it is really interesting to hear you say that, and I must confess something now. I was once addicted to drugs myself and only was able to be healed from it when I met God and had this experience of being born again. I believe the power of this experience and nothing else was able to shake me out of it. I have a very personal knowledge of the danger of drugs of any kind, so I am pleased to hear your very clear-cut response to it.

Continuing along the moral line, I would like to know how you feel about such things as explicit sex education and abortion on demand for minors regardless of parental disapproval. This seems to be an increasing trend, and we would like to know your thoughts on these areas.

Ronald Reagan: You have two thoughts there. One, I vetoed a bill that had to do with government making it possible for underage girls to get sex education or go to a doctor for contraceptive devices. I felt that this was government injecting itself into the very heart of the family, between parent and child. How dare government say something of this kind and keep it a secret between them and the child without (the) parents' knowledge! So, I vetoed that bill, but I believe it has since been signed into law by my successor.

On the matter of abortion, I have faced this problem with regard to legislation in my own state. I think it comes down to one simple answer that finally came to me . . . you cannot interrupt a pregnancy without taking a human life. And the only way we can justify taking a life in our Judeo-Christian tradition is in self-defense.

George Otis: That is a clear answer. I would like to talk about Korea. Korea is an interesting country, because it is one that has been visited by a great nationwide spiritual renewal. You may remember that Billy Graham spoke in Seoul, Korea, to a Christian congregation of over one million people. It was the largest Christian meeting in all history, and yet some American voices are now beginning to call for us to pull completely out of Korea, leaving them exposed. I am very interested in knowing what you would do about Korea.

Ronald Reagan: Korea is an ally. We have agreements and treaties with Korea . . . and we should make it plain to anyone who has adventurous ideas about aggression that we intend to maintain and keep our commitment to Korea.

George Otis: Governor Reagan, perhaps the most dramatic Bible prophecy which has been fulfilled right in our own day is the re-emergence of Israel as a nation. The Bible calls the Jews "chosen people," and it promises a blessing to those nations who bless the Jews. In view of this spiritual principle, what do you feel America should do if ever Israel was about to be destroyed by attacking enemy nations?

Ronald Reagan: Here again we have a relationship. We have a pledge to Israel for the preservation of that nation. They are an ally and have been a longtime friend. Again, we keep our commitment. I think there is a tendency today to go along with the things you were mentioning in our talk about "the easy way." There are many people taking advantage of the war weariness that came from the long conflict in Vietnam. There are many people who say that no agreement is worth keeping if it causes trouble to ourselves. We can't live that way. We have an obligation, a responsibility and a destiny. We are the leader of the free world and I think that to a certain extent in the last few years we have abdicated that leadership in a very definite withdrawal of moral commitments.

George Otis: It is almost as though people say, "Korea is so far away, and Israel is so far away, it really isn't any of our business. Why should we entangle ourselves?" It is kind of like Pilate of old who washed his hands and hoped it would go away. But it seems like these things are creeping closer and closer towards our doorstep.

Ronald Reagan: I have always wanted to ask someone if they were on this side of the street and . . . they saw someone abusing and beating up some defenseless person who couldn't take care of himself. They wouldn't think anything at all of crossing the street to help that person. Well, what difference does distance make? If it is just across the street, or across the ocean, or across a border, isn't the moral obligation the same? Did the good Samaritan measure the distance of the road before he crossed over?

George Otis: And the world is shrinking. With this as a factor, Korea isn't very far and Israel certainly isn't either. About the Bible, more and more people believe what the Bible really says about itself, that it has been given to mankind under the inspiration of God himself, yet others say it is merely a great collection of writings about ancient history, folklore and poetry. We would like to know what you believe and what the Bible really means to you.

Ronald Reagan: I have never had any doubt about it being of divine origin. And to those who . . . doubt it, I would like to have them point out to me any similar collection of writings that have lasted for as many thousands of years and is still the bestseller worldwide. It had to be of divine origin. How can you write off the prophecies in the Old Testament that hundreds of years before the birth of Christ predicted every single facet of His life, His death, and that He was the Messiah? They could say, "Well, they were fortunetellers and it was just luck."

George Otis: Too many are like that. Someone has said that about 20 percent of those 1265 Bible pages are prophetic, foretelling future events of the affairs of empires and millions of people. And they have come to pass as the Bible foretold. They have been just as God said they would be. The Bible does seem to be self-authenticating. It seems to be proving what it says about itself. It is very interesting to get your views on the Bible.

I would be interested to know if you have any particular Bible portion that is especially meaningful to you. Do you have any favorite section in the Bible?

Ronald Reagan: I once wrote a letter in which I gave verses two through five of Psalm 106. I don't know that I can confine my favorite passage to these few verses. As a matter of fact I think sometimes my favorite verses change with my needs. I have to say there have been times over the last few years when one passage alone, "Where two or more gather in my name, there shall I be also," has been a great comfort to me.

George Otis: Do you think He might be here with us right now? We are two gathered together in His name.

Ronald Reagan: I'd hate to think He wasn't.

George Otis: Would you mind reading that particular portion of the Word which is among your favorites?

Ronald Reagan: "Who can utter the mighty acts of the Lord? who can shew forth all his praise? Blessed are they that keep judgment, and he that doeth righteousness at all times. Remember me, O LORD, with the favour that thou bearest unto thy people: O visit me with thy salvation; That I may see the good of thy chosen, that I may rejoice in the gladness of thy nation, that I may glory with thine inheritance."

George Otis: Beautiful. I would like to ask you a question about prayer. You know prayer is a mysterious thing. And I would like to know if you think, in this highly intellectual age, that there really is any merit in prayer. Do you really believe somebody is listening up there?

Ronald Reagan: Oh, my! If I didn't believe that I'd be scared to death!

George Otis: Do you pray?

Ronald Reagan: Oh, yes I do.

George Otis: Have you ever had answers to prayer?

Ronald Reagan: Yes, I have.

George Otis: Would you give us one example, something personal?

Ronald Reagan: Well, there have been so many and some momentous ones. We talked a few moments ago about abortion. I had never given that much thought in my life. I never had occasion to. I am not of a church membership where the abortion issue is covered as a part of the doctrine. Finally, I arrived at an answer through a lot of soul-searching of my own. The legislator who had the bill sent word that he would amend it to whatever he felt I could sign. I finally arrived at the principle that I mentioned earlier. Abortion is taking a life, and this is wrong except in the case of self-defense. But I was still very concerned. Yes, I prayed that what I had done was the right decision.

Now that afternoon after I had given a word of what I could sign, a man came into my office on entirely different business. We concluded our business and as he started to leave he turned around and said, "Oh, I want to show you something." He reached in his briefcase and said, "I am on the board of an institution that helps children, dealing with those who are handicapped. Just this morning," he continued, "I was there and they had a little ceremony thanking me for some of the things that I had done.

Then one young lady presented me with this painting." He showed me one of the most beautiful landscapes I've seen in watercolors. Then he told me that the girl who painted it painted while holding the brush in her teeth. She was born without arms. I just refused to believe that on that particular day, that particular afternoon, that experience was just coincidence when I was so torn with regard as to whether I had made the right decision.

George Otis: It was pretty dramatic, wasn't it? It was like the Lord sent a telegram right back to you, wasn't it?

Ronald Reagan: Yes, it was.

George Otis: Let me ask you, did you pray, did you seek God, before you submitted yourself for candidacy for the most thankless job in the nation?

Ronald Reagan: Oh, my, yes.

George Otis: I have another question. I would like to know if you advocate astrology or horoscopes.

Ronald Reagan: I know where that question came from. I have run into this before. When I first became governor I was sworn in at one minute after midnight, and suddenly the rumors started that I did this because astrology told me this was when I should be sworn in. The answer wasn't anything quite so exotic. The simple truth was that my predecessor had held open about 325 judicial appointments to use them during the elections as bait. Then between the election and my inauguration he was daily appointing dozens of judges. I got so fed up with this since I was due to be inaugurated very shortly that I finally demanded to know . . . the first moment I could take the oath so he couldn't do this any more, and they told me one minute after midnight. I said, "That is when I will be sworn in."

George Otis: That is really a fascinating story.

As you become the leader of . . . the most prosperous nation in all history, how will you go about selecting leaders? Would you consider only the counsel of men or would you have . . . a blend of the counsel of men and seeking God's guidance on decisions?

Ronald Reagan: The latter, of course, I would have to do. When we did this in California and I became governor I often have told about one of the requirements. I didn't seek people who wanted government careers. I didn't want people who had a personal ambition for government. I wanted people who had actually considered it a service. They would be giving up a period of their lives to serve their fellow man and the community. And in addition, I don't want pragmatists. I don't want people who practice situational ethics. I would want people who abide by principle. I made a promise to myself in the campaign, and it still holds true. I kept that promise, and it was that every decision which I would have to make would be based on what was *morally* right or wrong. Not what was politically advantageous to anyone.

George Otis: I am convinced this will set a precedent. Every man who is running for high public office should be willing to sit and courageously respond to questions of character, principle and morals. One of the things that I know you are aware of, and I'm excited about, is the fact that this great spiritual revolution that has been occurring in our nation for the last five or ten years has begun to move upon the hearts of the people who have been silent so long. This silence has allowed the political processes in Washington to be neglected because of the mistaken idea that politics and religion don't mix. I am happy that there is a tremendous new wave that is causing these good and very able people to stand up and be interested and stand up for issues and the kind of people they are sending there. Do you believe Christians should make themselves available for public office?

Ronald Reagan: Certainly. Oh, yes. I have always said that one of the things the founding fathers never anticipated was professional politicians. I don't mean they are all bad. We have had great statesmen who have made careers out of government service, but I think that one of the reasons a congressional term is two years . . . is so that those who had served a stint or two in Congress would then go home and say, "All right, it is your turn. You work there." We have come to the place where there isn't enough outside influence in government. Now we've aggravated that with the professional bureaucrat who isn't even subject to change at the polls throughout his entire life. I think we've suffered that which Cicero called "the arrogance of official-dom."

George Otis: Teddy Roosevelt called the presidency the greatest pulpit in the nation. He felt that men who had a capability to exercise leadership in long-range, and not just short-range matters, was essential for the quality for the presidency. Would you use the presidency as a pulpit for leadership?

Ronald Reagan: Oh, I think that is long overdue. I think this is one of the things that is wrong. This hasn't happened since Franklin Delano Roosevelt. Whether people agreed with what he urged or not, he really took his case to the people over the head of government. Harry Truman once described the president as the only representative of all the people in Washington. He is the lobbyist for the people. He's the one man who represents the nation as a whole. The rest are either representing states or congressional districts. He represents the people, and my definition of leadership has been not necessarily one who does great things himself but one who can persuade others to do great things.

George Otis: The last question I would like to know is, if you have the privilege to be at the helm of the United States of America, do you envision yourself as being a president who would not only sit at his desk but one who would spend a fair amount of time on his knees?

Ronald Reagan: . . . Certainly the job in Washington would be impossible unless that man (the president) felt he could call on God for help knowing that help was forthcoming.

George Otis: Governor Reagan, it has been a high privilege to be with you. Thank you very much. God bless you.

George Otis
P.O. Box 7466
Van Nuys, CA 91409

APPENDIX B

The Reagan View of Abortion

RONALD REAGAN

July 27, 1979

The Honorable Henry J. Hyde
1203 Longworth House Office Building
House of Representatives
Washington, D.C. 20515

Dear Henry:

I want you to know that I have long admired your courage, determination and articulate championship of the vital cause of the unborn child in America today. I realize there is a great difference of opinion regarding the subject of abortion. People on both sides of this issue have very sincere, strongly held views.

I personally believe that interrupting a pregnancy is the taking of a human life and can only be justified in self-defense— that is, if the mother's own life is in danger.

In 1976 the Republican Party platform

protested the January 22, 1973 Supreme Court decision which overruled the historic role of the states in legislating in the areas concerning abortion and took away virtually every protection previously accorded the unborn. Later decisions have intruded into the family structure through their denial of the parents' obligations and right to guide their minor children. The platform called for a continuance of the public dialogue on abortion, and expressed support of the efforts of those who seek enactment of a constitutional amendment to restore protection of the right to life for unborn children.

I fully concur with our platform.

But the process of amending the Constitution is lengthy and difficult. As in other cases where I favor additions to our Constitution—to limit federal spending, and to balance the federal budget—my preference would be to first use the legislative process. If that fails, I would hope that Congress itself would propose the amendment and send it to the states for ratification. As a last resort I support the right of the people of the United States to call a consititutional convention for the specific purpose of proposing an amendment.

In the meantime, I am opposed to using federal tax money to pay for abortions in cases where the life of the mother is in no danger.

Sincerely,

RONALD REAGAN

APPENDIX C

The Candidate Talks About the SALT Treaty

OFFICE OF RONALD REAGAN
10960 Wilshire Boulevard
Los Angeles, California 90024
For information call:
Peter D. Hannaford
(231/477-8231)

EMBARGOED TILL
8:45 P.M. (PDT)
Saturday, September 15, 1979

SALT and the Search for Peace

EXCERPTS FROM REMARKS BY THE
HONORABLE RONALD REAGAN

REPUBLICAN STATE
CENTRAL COMMITTEE OF
CALIFORNIA CONVENTION
Town and Country Hotel
San Diego, California
Saturday, September 15, 1979

Over the past 15 years we have permitted the Soviet Union to deprive us of our nuclear advantage while at the same time it increased its superiority in conventional forces. Our once unrivaled advantage in naval strength is melting away, our fleet is shrinking almost as fast as theirs is growing.

Of what value can our commitments be if we are inferior both in nuclear and conventional forces? How do we support our friends and defend our vital interests in the Middle East? How do we protect our own freedom? And how in Heaven's name did we get in this perilous situation?

The wrong turn came 15 years ago when our own military resources were sucked into the war in Vietnam and our strategic defense budgets began to shrink year after year. We were entranced by the notion that if we pounded our swords into plowshares the Soviets would do likewise. They did exactly the opposite. While we made actual reductions in our strategic programs, they made massive investments in theirs.

Oh, they talked about arms control and seemed to hold out the promise of real progress. But somehow, progress was always just around the corner; just another American concession or two by us away from realization.

Our own Republican administrations should have reversed these policy assumptions. They should not have overstated what the Strategic Arms Limitation Talks could do for us. In 1972 we presented SALT I as a "turning point in the arms race," and began our reliance on what is called the "SALT Process," which included the doctrine of "Mutual Assured Destruction." At the same time, the Soviets began their exploitation of our naive desire to believe.

Toward the end of the last Republican administration the national mood had changed. There was repudiation of the defeatism of the Democrat-controlled Congress. We began a recovery of our military strength. The B-1 bomber was scheduled for production, the new MX missile was to be accelerated, the decline in our navy was to be reversed and many other urgent programs were set in motion.

All of these were reassuring to the American people. With the promise of long-range defense programs to provide for our security we went forward with the SALT II negotiations. But then came a new administration. The B-1 bomber was cancelled without any quid pro quo, the MX was slowed down, the cruise missile delayed, the Navy's ship-building program cut back and, under the heat of a Soviet propaganda attack, Mr. Carter halted development of a weapon that could have neutralized Russia's massive conventional superiority on the NATO front.

The Russians are now spending three times as much as we do on strategic arms and are increasing that by four to five percent a year. We are barely keeping pace with inflation. While Mr. Carter maintains that his defense programs for America are adequate, simple arithmetic tells us that the gap in military strength between us and the Soviets can only grow wider if we continue on our present course. The administration deceives the American people when it tells us the new SALT II agreement will put a brake on the arms race, save money and be adequately verifiable. SALT II is not Strategic Arms Limitation, it is a Strategic Arms Buildup, with the Soviets adding a minimum of 3,000 nuclear warheads to their inventory and the U.S. embarking on a $35 billion catchup which won't be achieved until 1990, if then.

The SALT treaty now before the Senate should not continue to monopolize our attention nor must it become the cause of a devisive political struggle. This is no time for Americans to quarrel among themselves. Our task is to restore the security of the U.S. and we should make it emphatically known to the Soviets and—more importantly—to the nations of the free world that we intend to do just that. At the same time, let us assure the Soviet Union we will join in any arms limitation agreement that legitimately reduces nuclear armaments to the point that neither country represents a threat to the other.

To suggest, as the administration has, that any shortcomings in this SALT II agreement can be rectified in continuing talks leading to a SALT III agreement is an exercise in futility. It makes no sense at all to ratify a Strategic Arms Limitation treaty that does not limit arms on either side but vastly increases them while at the same time we are told we'll enter into negotiations for a third such treaty that will make everything all right.

I believe the Senate should declare that this treaty, fatally flawed as it is, should be shelved and the negotiators should go back to the table and come up with a treaty which fairly and genuinely reduces the number of strategic nuclear weapons. And then the Senate should make up its mind on our policy on national security: Where are we going in the decade ahead? What are our obligations as leader of the free world and are we capable of meeting those obligations?

I respect the thinking of those senators and others who have suggested that the treaty, despite its weaknesses, could be approved as part of a "package" that would substantially strengthen our defense programs. But, I believe such a package deal would soon unravel and bring about the very dissension and confusion it was supposed to avoid. For one thing, it would send the wrong signal to the American people: it would create the impression that we are moving both up and down at the same time, and it would deceive more people than it would convince.

APPENDIX D

Reagan's Official Announcement

Official Announcement
November 13, 1979
7:30 P.M. (EST)
New York Hilton, New York, NY

Good evening. I am here tonight to announce my intention to seek the Republican nomination for President of the United States.

I'm sure that each of us has seen our country from a number of viewpoints depending on where we've lived and what we've done. For me it has been as a boy growing up in several small towns in Illinois. As a young man in Iowa trying to get a start in the years of the great depression and later in California for most of my adult life.

I've seen America from the stadium press box as a sportscaster, as an actor, officer of my labor union, soldier, officeholder and as both Democrat and Republican. I've lived in an America where those who often had too little to eat outnumbered those who had enough. There have been four wars in my lifetime and I've seen our country face financial ruin in the depression. I have also seen the great strength of this nation as it pulled itself up from that ruin to become the dominant force in the world.

To me our country is a living, breathing presence, unimpressed by what others say is impossible, proud of its own success, generous, yes and naive, sometimes wrong, never mean and always impatient to provide a better life for its people in a framework of a basic fairness and freedom.

Someone once said that the difference between an American and any other kind of person is that an American lives in anticipation of the future because he knows it will be a great place. Other people fear the future as just a repetition of past failures. There's a lot of truth in that. If there is one thing we are sure of it is that history need not be relived; that nothing is impossible, and that man is capable of improving his circumstances beyond what we are told is fact.

There are those in our land today, however, who would have us believe that the

United States, like other great civilizations of the past, has reached the zenith of its power; that we are weak and fearful, reduced to bickering with each other and no longer possessed of the will to cope with our problems.

Much of this talk has come from leaders who claim that our problems are too difficult to handle. We are supposed to meekly accept their failures as the most which humanly can be done. They tell us we must learn to live with less, and teach our children that their lives will be less full and prosperous than ours have been; that the America of the coming years will be a place where—because of our past excesses—it will be impossible to dream and make those dreams come true.

I don't believe that. And, I don't believe you do either. That is why I am seeking the presidency. I cannot and will not stand by and see this great country destroy itself. Our leaders attempt to blame their failures on circumstances beyond their control, on false estimates by unknown, unidentifiable experts who rewrite modern history in an attempt to convince us our high standard of living, the result of thrift and hard work, is somehow selfish extravagance which we must renounce as we join in sharing scarcity. I don't agree that our nation must resign itself to inevitable decline, yielding its proud position to other hands. I am totally unwilling to see this country fail in its obligation to itself and to the other free peoples of the world.

The crisis we face is not the result of any failure of the American spirit; it is a failure of our leaders to establish rational goals and give our people something to order their lives by. If I am elected, I shall regard my election as proof that the people of the United States have decided to set a new agenda and have recognized that the human spirit thrives best when goals are set and progress can be measured in their achievement.

During the next year I shall discuss in detail a wide variety of problems which a new administration must address. Tonight I shall mention only a few.

No problem that we face today can compare with the need to restore the health of the American economy and the strength of the American dollar. Double-digit inflation has robbed you and your family of the ability to plan. It has destroyed the confidence to buy and it threatens the very structure of family life itself as more and more wives are forced to work in order to help meet the ever-increasing cost of living. At the same time, the lack of real growth in the economy has introduced the justifiable fear in the minds of working men and women who are already overextended that soon there will be fewer jobs and no money to pay for even the necessities of life. And tragically as the cost of living keeps going up, the standard of living which has been our great pride keeps going down.

The people have not created this disaster in our economy; the federal government has. It has overspent, overestimated, and over-regulated. It has failed to deliver services within the revenues it should be allowed to raise from taxes. In the thirty-four years since the end of World War II, it has spent 448 billion dollars more than it has collected in taxes—448 billion dollars of printing-press money, which has made every dollar you earn worth less and less. At the same time, the federal government has cynically told us that high taxes on business will in some way "solve" the problem and allow the average taxpayer to pay less. Well, business is not a *taxpayer;* it is a *tax collector.* Business has to pass its tax burden on to the customer as part of the cost of doing business. You and I pay the taxes imposed on business every time we go to the store. Only *people* pay taxes and it is political demagoguery or economic illiteracy to try and tell us otherwise.

The key to restoring the health of the economy lies in cutting taxes. At the same time, we need to get the waste out of federal spending. This does not mean sacrificing essential services, nor do we need to destroy the system of benefits which flow to the poor, the elderly, the sick and the handicapped. We have long since committed ourselves, as a people, to help those among us who cannot take care of themselves. But the federal government has proven to be the costliest and most inefficient provider of such help we could possibly have.

We must put an end to the arrogance of a federal establishment which accepts no blame for our condition, cannot be relied upon to give us a fair estimate of our situation and utterly refuses to live within its means. I will not accept the supposed "wisdom" which has it that the federal bureaucracy has become so powerful that it can no longer be changed or controlled by any administration. As President I would use every power at my command to make the federal establishment respond to the will and the collective wishes of the people.

We must force the entire federal bureaucracy to live in the real world of reduced spending, streamlined functions and accountability to the people it serves. We must review the functions of the federal government to determine which of those are the proper province of levels of government closer to the people.

The 10th article of the Bill of Rights is explicit in pointing out that the federal government should do only those things specifically called for in the Constitution. All others shall remain with the states or the people. We haven't been observing that 10th article of late. The federal government has taken on functions it was never intended to perform and which it does not perform well. There should be a planned, orderly transfer of such functions to states and communities and a transfer with them of the sources of taxation to pay for them.

The savings in administrative overhead would be considerable and certainly there would be increased efficiency and less bureaucracy.

By reducing federal tax rates where they discourage individual initiative—especially personal income tax rates—we can restore incentives, invite greater economic growth and at the same time help give us better government instead of bigger government. Proposals such as the Kemp-Roth bill would bring about this kind of realistic reductions in tax rates.

In short, a punitive tax system must be replaced by one that restores incentive for the worker and for industry; a system that rewards initiative and effort and encourages thrift.

All these things are possible; none of them will be easy. But the choice is clear. We can go on letting the country slip over the brink to financial ruin with the disaster that it means for the individual or we can find the will to work together to restore confidence in ourselves and to regain the confidence of the world. I have lived through one depression. I carry with me the memory of a Christmas Eve when my brother and I and our parents exchanged our modest gifts—there was no lighted tree as there had been on Christmases past. I remember watching my father open what he thought was a greeting from his employer. We all watched and yes, we were hoping it was a bonus check. It was notice that he no longer had a job. And in those days the government ran radio announcements telling workers not to leave home looking for jobs—there were no jobs. I'll carry with me always the memory of my father sitting there holding that envelope, unable to look at us. I cannot and will not stand by while inflation and joblessness destroy the dignity of our people.

Another serious problem which must be discussed tonight is our energy situation. Our country was built on cheap energy. Today, energy is not cheap and we face the prospect that some forms of energy may soon not be available at all.

Last summer you probably spent hours sitting in gasoline lines. This winter, some will be without heat and everyone will be paying much more simply to keep home and family warm. If you ever had any doubt of the government's inability to provide for the needs of the people, just look at the utter fiasco we now call "the energy crisis." Not one straight answer nor any realistic hope of relief has come from the present administration in *almost three years* of federal treatment of the problem. As gas lines grew, the administration again panicked and now has proposed to put the country on a wartime footing; but for this "war" there is no victory in sight. And, as always, when the federal bureaucracy fails, all it can suggest is more of the same. This time it's another bureau to untangle the mess made by the ones we already have.

But, this *just won't* work. Solving the energy crisis will not be easy, but it can be done. First we must decide that "less" is not enough. Next, we must remove government obstacles to energy production. And, we must make use of those technological advantages we still possess.

It is no program simply to say "use less energy." Of course waste must be eliminated and efficiency promoted, but for the government simply to tell the people to conserve is not an energy policy. At best it means we will run out of energy a little more slowly. But a day will come when the lights will dim and the wheels of industry will turn more slowly and finally stop. As President I will not endorse any course which has this as its principal objective.

We need *more* energy and that means

diversifying our sources of supply away from the OPEC countries. Yes, it means more efficient automobiles. But it also means more exploration and development of oil and natural gas here in our own country. The only way to free ourselves from the monopoly pricing power of OPEC is to be less dependent on outside sources of fuel.

The answer obvious to anyone except those in the administration it seems, is more domestic production of oil and gas. We must also have wider use of nuclear power within strict safety rules, of course. There must be more spending by the energy industries on research and development of substitutes for fossil fuels.

In years to come solar energy may provide much of the answer but for the next two or three decades we must do such things as master the chemistry of coal. Putting the market system to work for these objectives is an essential first step for their achievement. Additional multi-billion dollar federal bureaus and programs are not the answer.

In recent weeks there has been much talk about "excess" oil company profits. I don't believe we've been given all the information we need to make a judgment about this. We should have that information. Government exists to protect us from each other. It is not government's function to allocate fuel or impose unnecessary restrictions on the marketplace. *It is* government's function to determine whether we are being unfairly exploited and if so to take immediate and appropriate action. As President I would do exactly that.

On the foreign front, the decade of the 1980s will place severe pressures upon the United States and its allies. We can expect to be tested in ways calculated to try our patience, to confound our resolve and to erode our belief in ourselves. During a time when the Soviet Union may enjoy nuclear superiority over this country, we must never waiver in our commitment to our allies nor accept any negotiation which is not clearly in the national interest. We must judge carefully. Though we should leave no initiative untried in our pursuit of peace, we must be clear-voiced in our resolve to resist any unpeaceful act wherever it may occur. Negotiation with the Soviet Union must never become appeasement.

For the most of the last forty years, we

have been preoccupied with the global struggle—the competition—with the Soviet Union and with our responsibilities to our allies. But too often in recent times we have just drifted along with events, responding as if we thought of ourselves as a nation in decline. To our allies we seem to appear to be a nation unable to make decisions in its own interests, let alone in the common interest. Since the Second World War we have spent large amounts of money and much of our time protecting and defending freedom all over the world. We must continue this, for if we do not accept the responsibilities of leadership, who will? And if no one will, how will we survive?

The 1970s have taught us the foolhardiness of not having a long-range diplomatic strategy of our own. The world has become a place where, in order to survive, our country needs more than just allies—it needs real friends. Yet, in recent times we often seem not to have recognized who our friends are. This must change. It is now time to take stock of our own house and to resupply its strength.

Part of that process involves taking stock of our relationship with Puerto Rico. I favor statehood for Puerto Rico and if the people of Puerto Rico vote for statehood in their coming referendum I would, as President, initiate the enabling legislation to make this a reality.

We live on a continent whose three countries possess the assets to make it the strongest, most prosperous and self-sufficient area on earth. Within the borders of this North American continent are the food, resources, technology and undeveloped territory which, properly managed, could dramatically improve the quality of life of all its inhabitants.

It is no accident that this unmatched potential for progress and prosperity exists in three countries with such long-standing heritages of free government. A developing closeness among Canada, Mexico and the United States—a North American accord—would permit achievement of that potential in each country beyond that which I believe any of them—strong as they are—could accomplish in the absence of such cooperation. In fact, the key to our own future security may lie in both Mexico and Canada becoming much stronger countries than they are today.

No one can say at this point precisely what form future cooperation among our three countries will take. But if I am elected President, I would be willing to invite each of our neighbors to send a special representative to our government to sit in on high level planning sessions with us, as partners, mutually concerned about the future of our Continent. First, I would immediately seek the views and ideas of Canadian and Mexican leaders on this issue, and work tirelessly with them to develop closer ties among our peoples. It is time we stopped thinking of our nearest neighbors as foreigners.

By developing methods of working closely together, we will lay the foundations for future cooperation on a broader and more significant scale. We will also put to rest any doubts of those cynical enough to believe that the United States would seek to dominate any relationship among our three countries, or foolish enough to think that the governments and peoples of Canada and Mexico would ever permit such domination to occur. I for one, am confident that we can show the world by example that the nations of North America are ready, within the context of an unswerving commitment to freedom, to seek new forms of accommodation to meet a changing world. A developing closeness between the United States, Canada and Mexico would serve notice on friend and foe alike that we were prepared for a long haul, looking outward again and confident of our future; that together we are going to create jobs, to generate new fortunes of wealth for many and provide a legacy for the children of each of our countries. Two hundred years ago we taught the world that a new form of government, created out of the genius of man to cope with his circumstances, could succeed in bringing a measure of quality of human life previously thought impossible.

Now let us work toward the goal of using the assets of this continent, its resources, technology and foodstuffs in the most efficient ways possible for the common good of all its people. It may take the next 100 years but we can dare to dream that at some future date a map of the world might show the North American continent as one in which the peoples and commerce of its three strong countries flow more freely across their present borders than they do today.

In recent months leaders in our government have told us that, we, the people, have lost confidence in ourselves; that we must regain our spirit and our will to achieve our national goals. Well, it is true there is a lack of confidence, an unease with things the way they are. But the confidence we have lost is confidence in our government's policies. Our unease can almost be called bewilderment at how our defense strength has deteriorated. The great productivity of our industry is now surpassed by virtually all the major nations who compete with us for world markets. And, our currency is no longer the stable measure of value it once was.

But there remains the greatness of our people, our capacity for dreaming up fantastic deeds and bringing them off to the surprise of an unbelieving world. When Washington's men were freezing at Valley Forge, Tom Paine told his fellow Americans: "We have it in our power to begin the world over again." We still have that power.

We—today's living Americans—have in our lifetime fought harder, paid a higher price for freedom and done more to advance the dignity of man than any people who ever lived on this earth. The citizens of this great nation want leadership—yes—but not a "man on a white horse" demanding obedience to his commands. They want someone who believes they *can* "begin the world over again." A leader who will unleash their great strength and remove the roadblocks government has put in their way. I want to do that more than anything I've ever wanted. And it's something that I believe with God's help I *can* do.

I believe this nation hungers for a spiritual revival; hungers to once again see honor placed above political expediency; to see government once again the protector of our liberties, not the distributor of gifts and privilege. Government should uphold and not undermine those institutions which are custodians of the very values upon which civilization is founded—religion, education and, above all, family. Government cannot be clergyman, teacher and parent. It is our servant, beholden to us.

We who are privileged to be Americans have had a rendezvous with destiny since the moment in 1630 when John Winthrop, standing on the deck of the tiny *Arbella* off the coast of Massachusetts, told the little band of Pilgrims, "We shall be as a city upon a hill. The eyes of all people are upon us so that if we shall deal falsely with our God in this work we have undertaken and so cause Him to withdraw His present help from us, we shall be made a story and a byword throughout the world."

A troubled and afflicted mankind looks to us, pleading for us to keep our rendezvous with destiny; that we will uphold the principles of self-reliance, self-discipline, morality, and—above all—responsible liberty for every individual; that we will become that shining city on a hill.

I believe that you and I together can keep this rendezvous with destiny.

Thank you and good night.

APPENDIX E

The Candidate on the State of the Economy

REAGAN FOR PRESIDENT
9841 Airport Boulevard
Suite 1430
Los Angeles, California 90045

EMBARGOED UNTIL:
1:30 P.M. (EST)
Tuesday, April 8, 1980

CONTACT:
Ed Gray, Press Secretary
traveling with Ronald Reagan
or
Joe Holmes: 213-670-9161

REMARKS BY
RONALD REAGAN
Tuesday, April 8, 1980
American Society of Newspaper Editors
Washington Hilton Hotel
Washington, D.C.

There are several things that set the 1980 Presidential campaign apart from all others. This year, by the time we're finished, there will have been 37 primaries. By contrast, just 20 years ago, there was only a handful of them and it took the Democrats two to determine their nominee.

But the 1980's differences only begin there. Already, we are seeing a reversal of a 20-year downward trend in voter turnout. This year, for example, more people voted in the Massachusetts, Iowa, New Hampshire and Illinois primaries than ever before. I'm happy to see that in many primaries the Republicans are setting new records for voter participation. That's encouraging and says something positive about the competitive testing process which the primaries represent.

Out on the campaign trail, where I've been for all but a few days of the last 13 weeks, I'm often asked in interviews by members of your profession how I can appeal across party lines, to Democrats and Independents. It was, after all, another Republican candidate who was supposed to have "crossover appeal." In retrospect, it seems that those who were saying this were thinking in terms of traditionally *liberal* Democrats who found no candidate in their own party satisfying. What they had overlooked was that a different sort of crossover was actually beginning to take place; one that may foreshadow a major change in American politics. This is the crossover voting of increasing numbers of blue-collar workers, ethnics, registered Democrats and Independents with conservative values. Am I happy to have these votes? Of course I am, yes, and the Republican party will need millions of them in November.

The day of appeals to group interests alone is fast disappearing. We are seeing a growing determination on the part of voters to be seen not just as members of economic groups or social classes, but as human beings with values they hold dear. On the farm, in labor unions, on the street corners of the cities and in white-collar offices; in the suburbs (where the values of the old neighborhoods have been preserved) and in the old neighborhoods themselves, there is the new coalition, and I believe it is coming our way.

Political experts used to tell us that there were social issues and economic issues. Today, the economic issues are *the* primary social issue. The economic disaster confronting us hurts family values, destroys family savings and eats away at the very heart of family hopes and dreams. We can and should treat this economic disaster—brought on by those here in Washington who pay lip service to the family—as an ethical as well as an economic problem. We have economic problems because the Carter administration and some in Congress have not faced the truth.

We are paying for that today in the form of ruinous inflation and in Mr. Carter's latest economic policies which are a recipe for recession. He blames the working man and woman of this nation for his administration's shortcomings.

Conventional wisdom has it that it is bad politics to try to appeal, with the same message, to different groups. But why should we tell one group one thing and another group another. Most Americans share the same hopes and, today, the same fears.

In state after state we are finding that our campaign is in the process of breaking down artificial barriers that for too long kept Americans with shared values but with different economic, social or geographical backgrounds away from each other in terms of political action.

To all of them—in the union halls and in the office building; to the cop on the beat, the shopkeeper and the worker who is trying to do a job—the message of this campaign is simply this:

For too long your values—the values of the family, neighborhood, work, peace-through-strength and freedom-through-vigilance—have been mocked and ignored and exploited. The Washington bureaucrats and the Congressional majority have picked your pocket through inflation, bussed your children and ridiculed your desire for a strong national defense. Your desire to live a peaceful, decent life has been scorned because you didn't go along with their utopian schemes to remake society.

This is a new coalition of shared values and I believe its time has come. The values of this, the American middle class, should be deeply involved in the decision-making process in Washington, for these values underlie the strength of our nation. Yet, we have entered a time when those in positions of leadership tell us over and over again that the best has come and gone; that we must do with less. To those who have always had less—especially the minorities—this is like saying that just as you are about to board the train it has left the station.

Right now the most important issue we Americans face is this: can we stop inflation and still enjoy economic growth and a rising standard of living? Or, as our leaders are telling us, must we endure a mixture of high inflation, unemployment, austerity and limited unemployment for an indefinite period?

I believe we have the knowledge to devise policies that will stop inflation, restore vitality to our economy, and provide private employment for all willing Americans. We certainly know that today's policies have not worked. The present administration does not seem to know or to believe that the American people have the will to succeed. There is a noisy element—especially in government—which argues that growth itself is either undesirable or impossible; that an individual should no longer strive to climb the ladder of opportunity; that a parent wanting to make life better for his or her family is somehow misguided. To that element, the idea of "no-growth" or "limited growth" has become an end in itself.

But that makes sense only to those who are satisfied to remain where they are, and happy to see those below them remain where they are. But none of that makes sense to the people I've been talking to.

Most Americans still favor the growth of individual potential. Whatever it is we want to do—care for the old and needy, protect our natural and historical heritage, defend our freedoms or otherwise improve the quality of American life—our nation's economic growth is a prerequisite.

Our leaders seem to be saying that America's time of greatness is past; that Americans have become self-indulgent; that our country was built on cheap energy and abundant natural resources which are no longer available.

These are the arguments of despair. I reject them and I believe the American people reject them. This country was built on the hard work, thrift and ingenuity of its people. Surely we have at least as much *human initiative* in this country as we have ever had. There is no shortage of either natural or human resources which is not caused by the ill-advised policies of our own government. We can develop our resources, if government will let us.

In the next few minutes let me outline the strategy I think we shall need to stop inflation and to get the nation moving forward again. I propose no gimmicks. When a nation has been as badly managed as ours, it is time to get back to basics.

For almost 200 years, as we Americans expanded the world's economic and spiritual frontiers, we asked just three things of our government: to protect us from internal disorder, to assume our national security and to maintain a strong, stable dollar at home and abroad. We accepted sensible taxes and regulations to advance our national goals without hindering productivity and initiative. And, we demanded that the government balance its books and pay back outstanding debts during peacetime.

If the government would do those things, we would do the rest.

For almost two centuries, the United States was the world's model of government, a "shining city on a hill" whose success showed the rest of the world that democracy can provide every citizen the chance to reach as high or as far as skill, talent and industry will take him or her.

But, this formula of success has been put aside in more recent years. The stable dollar was replaced by the idea that a little inflation is good for the economy. Taxes and regulations multiplied beyond reason,

along with their indispensable handmaid-
en, the bureaucracy. And, prompt repay-
ment of our debts was replaced by the
notion that government borrowing is a
positive virtue.

We can see the results of these changes.
The dollar has shrunk to 43 cents compared
to the 1967 dollar. Our standard of living
has fallen behind that of other nations and
continues to decline. Inflation continues its
relentless march—now about 20 percent—
and American productivity is declining.
Yet, our government not only refuses to
look inward for the cause of our problems,
it goes on to blame the American people.
The Administration says we have inflation
because Americans expect too much out of
life. The President says we are less productive because we are losing our confidence.

The President's economic advisers have
estimated that to reduce inflation by a single percentage point, they must eliminate
the wages of about two million workers.
Either that many people must lose their
jobs, or else that much must be deducted
from everyone's income with taxes and
wage controls.

If that scares you, it should. The government is saying that to get inflation down to

where it was only four years ago, more people would have to lose their jobs than at any time during the Great Depression.

The administration's approach doesn't make sense and that is why inflation has doubled since Mr. Carter began his series of so-called "anti-inflation" policies. Inflation is not caused by workers or businessmen or consumers or producers. It is not like a plague of locusts or by mysterious forces from outer space. It is caused by government. The price of goods can go up only if the government creates too many dollars. Deficits tempt it to print new dollars instead of paying back its debt with honest money. We must remove that temptation by curbing government's appetite and by balancing the budget.

Of course, getting control of the government's monetary policy is only part of the answer to inflation. We also need strong economic growth. When we produce fewer goods, prices go up, not down. Yet, that is precisely the course Mr. Carter has chosen.

It is right that we worry about declining productivity. Higher productivity means we can produce more with the same effort. It takes people who have better ideas. And, it takes people with savings to invest in those ideas. It also takes motivated workers to turn those ideas into the reality of products and services. You can't increase productivity by making people work harder for less pay. They need better tools and rewards equal to their effort.

The federal income tax is a tax on all individual productivity—on labor, on savings and investment, on enterprise. These tax rates climb steeply with income. But, what's worse, they are not adjusted for inflation. Every time inflation raises your income, but not your buying power, you are pushed into a higher tax bracket. Over the past decade, this combination of inflation and steep tax rates has reduced the reward for higher productivity—for both individuals and for business.

I don't think anyone objects to paying reasonable taxes. And, we all agree on the need to help the less fortunate, but, rich or poor, young or old, a person's reward for working *more* should always clearly exceed his reward for working *less*.

The government's refusal to adjust (or "index") income tax rates for inflation not only stops all Americans from climbing higher on the economic ladder, it also pushes some people off the bottom rung every year. Two million more Americans are considered permanently unemployed today than only 10 years ago.

Those who do manage to keep their grip on the ladder still face dismal prospects. In half of the households, rich and poor alike, the government takes at least 50 cents of every one-dollar wage or salary increase, and the average is 46 cents. At these rates, you need to increase your income about twice as fast as inflation just to stay even after taxes.

Americans aren't losing their confidence, they're losing their shirts!

What about Mr. Carter's statement awhile back that Americans worship consumption and are unwilling to save for the future? Is this why they saved less of their income last year than in 30 years? With inflation well into double digits, even with the latest proposals to increase savings interest rates, anyone who does save is losing money. Not only does the government tax the interest on savings, further reducing their value, now the Administration wants to withhold that tax at the source, creating more work for bureaucrats and increasing government's share of those earnings by an estimated 2 to 2½ billion dollars.

But what happens if, against all odds, you succeed in really putting something away? Suppose you want to form an investment large enough to provide a continuing source of income for your family when you are gone. Or, want to leave a family-owned business or a farm? At today's inflated prices that family-owned business or farm will have to be sold to pay inheritance taxes.

To me, that's wrong. It's one thing for the government to tax a family's income, but it's something else to force that family to liquidate its *source* of income, just so the government can spend the proceeds. And this tax can hardly be justified on the basis of government's need; gift and estate taxes raise barely one percent of all federal revenue.

Americans as individuals produce more than four-fifths of the national income. But all of us are also seriously affected by the government's combination of inflation, unproductive taxes and heavy regulations on business.

Like the income tax, our outdated corporation tax does not adjust for inflation. A businessman may not allow for the rising cost of replacing plant, machinery and inventories. The result: inflation causes profits to be taxed at too high a rate.

At the same time, compliance with mushrooming government regulations adds $100 billion a year to the cost of doing business and therefore to the cost of living.

These, then are the major flaws in our economy. There is no crisis of confidence; no collapse of the American spirit. What we are suffering from is misguided, thoughtless government policies. Our government has nothing to show for them but economic decline and wasteful spending, despite much recent bluster about budget balancing. If those $15 billion worth of items can be cut from Mr. Carter's recently presented "austere" budget, why were they there in the first place?

We don't need to abolish government or its safety net of programs. But, we must change the government's policies to get it working on our side rather than against us.

I would tell our monetary authorities that they have only one job: to restore and maintain a sound dollar at home and abroad. They would be directed to create as few or as many dollars as it will take to stabilize the value of what a dollar will buy.

In proceeding toward the goal of full employment without inflation, I would ask Congress to act immediately to begin the necessary reform of our tax system; to restore the rewards for working and saving by cutting income tax rates and adjusting them automatically for inflation. My goal would be to cut the tax rates of all Americans by at least 30 percent over three years. And, I would ask Congress to widen the tax brackets yearly thereafter to prevent any further tax "bracket creep" caused by inflation.

I believe Congress should also help existing businesses with measures designed, at a minimum, to adjust corporate tax rates for inflation. It is only fair that businesses be allowed to account for the true cost of replacing their plant, equipment and inventories. This is necessary if American business is to recover and to stand up to the fierce international competition of the 1980s.

As to federal gift and estate taxes, I believe they should be abolished. The federal government never imposed such death taxes, except in emergencies, until the Depression. Before that, this property-tax base traditionally belonged to the states.

Is it only coincidence that the number of farms in this country has dropped every year for 44 years straight since the estate tax rates were first hoisted to their current level?

As the third aspect of this program, I would go after excessive federal spending. A freeze on federal hiring would be one step. Seeking out and eliminating waste and fraud would be another. Last year, the present Attorney General, before he assumed that post, told Congress that something between one and 10 percent of the federal budget could be estimated to fall into these categories. At the time, that meant as much as $50 billion. Likewise, inflation adds to the government's cost. It is estimated that every one percent of inflation increases spending about $5 billion. Every one percentage point added to the unemployment rate costs the government between 25 and 29 billion dollars.

As part of the process of streamlining government, we should take a close look at the efficiency of various federal programs to determine which could be handled more effectively by state and local government. Those that can should be transferred—in an orderly, phased manner—along with the tax sources to pay for them. I believe there would be a tremendous savings in administrative overhead. Welfare is one major prospect for such transfer. In California, where we were able to put a major reform program into effect, we reduced the rolls, saved the taxpayers added expense and still increased grants to those truly in need by an average of 43 percent.

It's a big job to turn a government around, and it must be done with care. But, it must be done.

Critics of major tax cuts usually cry that these will aggravate inflation by enlarging the federal deficit. They don't take into account the fact that the additional money the people get to keep isn't buried in a tin can in the backyard. It's put into savings and investments; into a new car; a vacation; a new room on the house—all the things people do when they make decisions in the marketplace. That money spreads out through the economy. It means more production so there would be more jobs. And, both the prospect of reality of tax cuts would have a positive effect on the nation's investment markets.

Recent history shows that significant tax cuts, rather than throwing sand in the gears of the federal machinery, actually help it. For the five years just prior to the round of tax cuts proposed by President Kennedy's administration, federal tax receipts increased by 25 percent. But, during the five years they were taking effect, federal receipts increased by more than 50 percent! Inflation wasn't a factor. During the earlier five-year period it averaged only 1.6 percent, and only 2.3 percent during the second period. A more productive economy produced the added revenue.

Similar effects were seen when major tax cuts were put into effect by the Harding and Coolidge administrations in the twenties.

The program I am talking about is not a "free lunch," but a plan for economic growth. We must have growth. Other nations have not waited, militarily or economically, for the United States to squabble over matters that should have been settled long ago. The world is a more dangerous and challenging place today than when our leaders turned inward to debate whether America would continue to be great. We have no choice but to be great. The world has never begged more clearly for us to serve as its shining city on a hill, a place of refuge, as well as an example and proof of democracy's strength.

Today, even though our nation's security has been allowed to greatly deteriorate, my confidence in the strength and patriotism of the American people remains unshaken. But, we cannot meet our world responsibilities without a strong economic policy which is effective both at home and in the world marketplace.

The Carter administration explains away much of our inflation as caused by the need to import oil. Yet, we import less than half of what we use. Germany imports 96 percent and Japan 100, yet their inflation rates are only a fraction of ours. As a result, their industry invests more in capital equipment and research and their governments take only two-thirds the percentage of total output in taxes as ours does.

A productive new economic program can make it possible for us to restore our competitiveness and our defense capabilities. And, armed with the knowledge that we are putting our economic house in order we can again gain the confidence of our friends and allies around the world. The conduct of American foreign policy is essentially a task of effectively managing our resources—material, human and moral—and implementing policies which use those resources in the pursuit of our national interest.

I began these remarks by commenting on the new coalition I see forming in American politics: a coalition of people with shared values and a desire to put them to work productively. So, too, on a global scale, once we act again as the leaders of the free world, I believe we will be supported by a grand coalition of other nations and peoples who want to work with us to preserve their freedom.

Here in America our choice is not between liberal and conservative, young and old, black and white, rich and poor, Sunbelt and Snowbelt, consumer and producer, or Democrat and Republican. No, our choice is between up and down; up to the ultimate in individual freedom, consistent with an orderly society, or down through statism and government intervention to authoritarianism or even totalitarianism. And, to me, the signs are everywhere and they are unmistakable—the American people want to go up.

Thank you.

This book available in case lots (50 in a case) through local bookstores or write for information:

Haven Books
201 Church Street
Plainfield, N.J. 07060

Ask for case lot price for *Reagan in Pursuit of the Presidency—1980*